THE RAPTURE OF EDDY DAEMON
(A POSTHUMAN HOMAGE TO
SHAKE-SPEARES SONNETS) 1-3-19

To my dear Friend, Norman —
thank you for your support
and friendship these last
several years —
    talk about " the Hotel
            url " —

Books by Daniel Y. Harris

The Underworld of Lesser Degrees
(NYQ Books, 2015)

Hyperlinks of Anxiety
(Cervena Barva Press, 2013)

Unio Mystica
(Cross-Cultural Communications, 2009)

Collaborative Books by Daniel Y. Harris

The Co-ordinates of Doubt
(with Rupert M. Loydell, The Knives Forks and Spoons Press, 2016)

Di./um
(with Irene Koronas, Smallminded Books, 2016)

Esophagus Writ
(with Rupert M. Loydell, The Knives Forks and Spoons Press, 2014)

X & F Metamorphosis
(with Walter Ruhlmann, et al, mgv2>publishing, 2014)

The New Arcana
(with John Amen, NYQ Books, 2012)

Paul Celan and the Messiah's Broken Levered Tongue: An Exponential Dyad
(with Adam Shechter, Cervena Barva Press, 2010)

Blurbs of Praise for **The Rapture of Eddy Daemon**

Finally: a posthuman translation of Shakespeare. I'm glad Daniel Y. Harris beat Watson at it. There are still large chunks of human in his kind lineation."

—Andrei Codrescu, author of *Bibliodeath: My Archives (with Life in Footnotes)*, (Antibookclub, 2012)

In *The Rapture of Eddy Daemon*, Daniel Y. Harris has composed a wild poetic drama through realms of eros and spirituality. His writing is simultaneously playful and profound, transmuting ancient symbols and concepts into a contemporary wisdom, heretofore unknown in poetry.

—Daniel C. Matt, author of the first nine volumes of the annotated translation, *The Zohar: Pritzker Edition*, and of *The Essential Kabbalah*, and *God and the Big Bang*

Daniel Y. Harris has a perfect ear. *Pass it on.* "It's the last season of day one." Crisp consonants frame smart vowels betwixt parentheses that host deliciously true songs. Whole verse thrums from peak to sprawl. He crafts high-frequency fluidity. Each sonnet is agleam with future friction, "revers(ing) this law of creation." The litmus state, "Unborn in choiring wings," reminds us that "The topos is in the billions." Each fleck of this multiplicative joy ride earns a resounding "YES"!

—Sheila E. Murphy, author of more than 30 books of poetry, including *Letters to Unfinished J.*, winner of the Gertrude Stein Award by Green Integer Press, and *Continuations* (with Douglas Barbour), co-founded the Scottsdale Center for the Arts Poetry Series.

Though last words are rarely included in blurbs, Jack Spicer's "My vocabulary did this to me" is apt praise for Daniel Y. Harris' linguistic tour de force, *The Rapture of Eddy Daemon*, which is a procedural and meta-linguistic commentary on Shakespeare's sonnets and so much more—from Faustian saga of human creation to an ode to the mechanical and posthuman methods of gaining access once again to the imagination. The circle/cycle is unbroken and broken simultaneously—and that is the joy of this big, ambitious, and brilliant riff on what "revision," at its most exuberant boundary can mean. Read this forever and then start again.

—Maxine Chernoff, author of *Here* (Counterpath) and *To Be Read in the Dark* (Omnidawn), is Chair of the San Francisco State University Creative Writing Department.

The fourteen-line sonnet form is the setting for this epic homage to the Bard. Harris' bold achievement is nothing less than a sustained ecstatic idiom—a *combinatoria*, encyclopaedic in range, via which this *daemon*, this genius, this attendant spirit he calls *Daemon* eddies uninhibitedly.

—Gregory Vincent St. Thomasino, author of *The Valise* and Editor of E·ratio

To be Human or... Posthuman? That is the question Daniel Y. Harris asks in *The Rapture of Eddy Daemon*, his new techno-savvy collection; an alluring post-avant garde 'frieze of parabola and rosaries... eccentricities and personae'. Outraged critics may balk at the *esthétique du mal* infusing this neon-lit sonnet-homage to the Bard, but disregard their slings and arrows – just fasten your seatbelt for this white-knuckle ride through a multifaceted New Inscape of poetic phantasmagorical visuality.

—AC Evans is the author of *Fractured Moods* (Atlantean Publishing, 2012), *From Outside* (Argotist e-books, 2012) and *Vespula Vanishes and Other Poems* (Inclement Publishing, 2007)

The originality of Daniel Y. Harris' writings is a multilayered surprisal, one of joyful momentum and challenging nuances that alters the reader's understanding of language. In essence, one of the gifts of *The Rapture of Eddy Daemon* is its ability to advocate for poetic language, but too, for language in a general contextual awareness. This superb collection will create neoteric discernment for the reader ready to delve beyond what is currently being written. Harris has created, through Daemon's interaction, something very new and deliberate, —something truthful into the paradigm of what creates rapture and its subsequent experiences.

—Felino A. Soriano, author of *sparse anatomies of single antecedents,* is the Founder/Publisher of *Counterexample Poetics* and *Of/*with: journal of immanent renditions.

THE RAPTURE OF EDDY DAEMON
(A POSTHUMAN HOMAGE TO
SHAKE-SPEARES SONNETS)

DANIEL Y. HARRIS

BLAZEVOX[BOOKS]
Buffalo, New York

Printed in the United States of America

Interior design and typesetting by Geoffrey Gatza
Cover Art: The Rapture of Eddy Daemon
Mixed-Media Sculpture (Detail of Head)
Artwork Copyright © Daniel Y. Harris, 2001
Photograph © Ed Bettencourt, 2001

First Edition
ISBN: 978-1-60964-254-9
Library of Congress Control Number: 2016935833

BlazeVOX [books]
131 Euclid Ave
Kenmore, NY 14217

Editor@blazevox.org

publisher of weird little books

BlazeVOX [books]

blazevox.org

21 20 19 18 17 16 15 14 13 12 01 02 03 04 05 06 07 08 09 10

BlazeVOX

Dedication

for Carre and Hans

Introductory Quotes

Not marble, nor the gilded monuments
Of princes, shall outlive this powerful rhyme;
But you shall shine more bright in these contents
Than unswept stone besmear'd with sluttish time.
When wasteful war shall statues overturn,
And broils root out the work of masonry,
Nor Mars his sword nor war's quick fire shall burn
The living record of your memory.
'Gainst death and all-oblivious enmity
Shall you pace forth; your praise shall still find room
Even in the eyes of all posterity
That wear this world out to the ending doom.
 So, till the judgment that yourself arise,
 You live in this, and dwell in lover's eyes.

—William Shakespeare
SHAKE-SPEARES SONNETS, LV

I trembled, and my heart failed within me; when, on looking up, I saw, by the light of the moon, the daemon at the casement. A ghastly grin wrinkled his lips as he gazed on me, where I sat fulfilling the task which he had allotted to me. Yes, he had followed me in my travels; he had loitered in forests, hid himself in caves, or taken refuge in wide and desert heaths; and he now came to mark my progress, and claim the fulfillment of my promise.

—Mary Shelley
Frankenstein, or The Modern Prometheus

The Daemon is neither a mythological deus ex machina, nor a simple task-oriented machine. In many ways, it sets the ground for redefining artificial intelligence and our current "modern" concepts of space, and it does this by blurring the lines between myth, literature, philosophy, anthropology, science, and technology.

—Chris Seroquel
The Daemon and Heidegger's Enframing

If the process is started by a super server daemon, such as "inetd," "launchd", or "systemd," the super-server daemon will perform those functions for the process (except for old-style daemons not converted to run under "systemd" and specified as Type=forking and "multi-threaded" datagram servers "underinetd").

—Michael C. St. Johns
Identification Protocol, "RFC1413"

Acknowledgement

Grateful acknowledgement is made to the editors of the following publications, in which poems in this volume first appeared, sometime in earlier versions:

Backlash Journal: "Antipersonnel 1,200–1,310 ft/s (370–400 m/s)," "Geisha 794," "Nym 7"

Big Bridge: "Stem 200," "Extinct 3079," "Intromit 7.9," "Tika 91"

BlazeVOX: "Usher 1839," "Sequitur 2015," "Fatale 69," "Carthaginian 146," "Chaetophobia 342"

E·ratio: "Decalogue 10," "Mali T624GPU," "ISBN 978-0-9883713-4-7," "Sonnetto 154," "Ratio 4:3," "X-Peri 5.0," "Bunjie 5.1," "Orb 5.2," "Pook 5.3," "Te./po 5.4"

experiential-experimental-literature: "Invokevirtual #85; //Methodjava/io/PrintStream.println:(I)V," and "Range 95-99%+"

First Literary Review—East: "Gross 15.89"

Grey Sparrow Journal: "Dow 16,544.10>115.15 (0.69%)," "Retrieve 2006"

International Times—The Newspaper of Resistance: "Melancholy 1514," "Necrotic 1952," "Vesper 1662," "Mediocrity 2.7

The Helios Mss: "Morse 1923"

The HIV Here & Now Project: "Pansexual 1917," "Rarity 88"

Hot Tub Astronaut: "Suicidium 801"

Levure Littéraire: "Bokor 1932," "Eve 99,000," "Kalashnikov 7.62×39"

MadHat Lit: "Legacy 0.0086%," "Vendredi 13"

mgv2>publishing, Daniel Y. Harris & Friends, Metamorphosis: "Redeemer 787," "Nicaea 325," "Creation 32," "Liber 777," "Curlicue $x^2 + 3x - 4 = (x + 4)(x - 1) = 0$," "Cosmographicum 1596"

mgversion2>datura: "Promethazine 00603-1585-58," "Sertraline 68180-0352-02"

Nerve Damage: A Booklet Anthology of Poems in Response to Joel-Peter Witkin's Photograph 'The Poet:' "Man 1480"

New Mystics: "Stonehenge 108," "Commandment 613," "Metron 6000," "Cipher 0," "Monad IX," "Wunderkind 1962," "Ubu 1896," "Denkstätte 1945"

Of/with: journal of immanent renditions: "Tenebrae $A^2 + B^2 = C^2$," "Digamma 13:17-18," "Reprise C/FF#9+D/GFSUS2/AB," "Écouté 1791," "Modal 1961," "Chiroptera 777," "Limbic 53," "Lemma $2^{32} \approx 4 \times 10^9$," "Beacon 417," "La Plume 1868," "Designate LII5A3," "Coulomb 1.602×10^{-19}," "Manji 90," "Foudre 12305," "Job 1:6," "Golem 139:16," "Ham 1602," "Alchemy 1606," "Offspring F1," "Kippur 5776"

Offcourse Literary Journal: "Ascent 30," "Dormition 15," "Lefe.ty 917"

Otoliths: "Adonis 600," "Icon 1700," "Jest 1996," "Hewoma 2.8," "Duchess 415"

PoetryMagazine.com: "Lodge 99"

Ragazine: "Mathewson 11," "Danger 1026," "Mandy 1972"

Rasputin: A Poetry Thread: "Scheherazade 1001," "Nebuchadnezzar 587,"

"Anthropoid 3761"

Five Pure Slush Vol. 10: "Alphanumeric XYZV>5"

The Somerville Times: "Hyle $i^2 = -1$"

Stride: "Scatotheological 1," "Helix 2," "Clarithromycin 68382-0762-14", "Apocalypse 5775," "Revelation 17:14–18," "Apology 399," "Coefficient .916," "Grimm 209," "Sequester 11%,"

Visual Verse: An Anthology of Art and Words: "Vacate 60"

Wilderness House Literary Review: "Beast 666," "Helix 144," "Subatomic 13.798," "Mandelbrot 3.14159," "Zoas 4"

Ygdrasil, a Journal of the Poetic Arts: "Babalú 401," "Cluster 34," "Emoji 12×12," "Cast 2237," "Esperanto 1895," "Listener 150%," "Capet 16"

Table of Contents

THE RAPTURE OF EDDY DAEMON
(A POSTHUMAN HOMAGE TO
SHAKE-SPEARES SONNETS)

Beast 666

Finger-taut grip of blue-black veins—collusion
mixed with envy, linked to us as Eddy Daemon's
gross motor skills with glassy eyes and clammy
palms declaim his end with App. He's in repose's
lack turning into us. He begins to scale the tiers,
a dark hint to forebear in dread and hear blanks
in the tropes of expiry. It's the vitriol of a partial
eclipse following him in rank dress with autopsy.
No excess translation of shriveled form cloaked
thin at the Ectomorph Gala. Once and for all, we
admit that Eddy Daemon is a hauntboy, a puerile
ephebe: vital, arrogant, fatal and dominant tri/X.
We know the xy/rills. Light saurces lit obscurote
with flick-bonez of a darkori, gutted self in neon.

Commandment 613

This odd morphology of regret is his killjoy,
blackburied and data burnt in effigy, gorging
in captivity, dethroned, seizing the obscured,
misidentified apostrophe. Eddy's derived like us
from an *esthétique du mal*, is a philandering anti,
teary sentimentalist, airy romantic, dark-blooded
in rugged hallow and brainspin. He's also vacant
as a shaken realist, thick-lidded with prophecies
of a copycat mood killer, listening to our filial
resentment. His negation has always been lit
by eccentricities and *personae*. It's never mere
panic or nostalgia for a past of fake halcyon
days. He's not driven by a pedagogical anima.
He's, *au fond*, our savage severity and copout.

Redeemer 787

Disentropic, he's unperplexed by malformed
jeers and metaslurs, mauled by obese halos
of cunning as exploited *paisant* against stale slack
and hack. Ransack Eddy's divestiture. We're his
aliases. He's incognito, a garnish of nostalgia pâtés
and red-jellied, *chaud-froid* aspic in a terracotta
terrine. Was it unpeopled? The *beshert* moment,
we mean, with a blast of flats, was that unpeopled,
or did Eddy beg to be picked vizier of a gang
of eschatologists? No, he's linked and lacquered,
sun-berated, wind-slandered, fog-dissed, in spells
of promethazine with codeine, hydrocodone
and levofloxacin. To hell with self-mastery
and the *ostent evanescent* choked with shit.

Nicaea 325

Paved aisles of carnelian stone, sard and ivory,
perched above the Jezreel Valley and Mount Tabor,
try to deter his attention deficit disorder in parquet
and lozenge shaped openings. He tries falling
sideways up with protosinaic eclogues, butchers
decrepit analogues, ashamed to confess he feels
nothing. For our sake, let's here redact "nothing"
to "the mortification of the flesh" and add barcode.
Presto, the bylaws have been amended. A cilice?
Yes, a punk hairshirt of sackcloth and syringes.
In the prequel, the cilice is metal with inward
pointing spikes: Eddy as seven demons of Mary
Magdalene and Brown's albino numerary, Silas.
Our welcome is a dismissal of polite induction.

Scheherazade 1001

The logic of a base is misnomer and defamation.
Eddy overrehearses his garage band, *Libido
of Eunuch's* antipop single "Butt Crud Harbinger,"
grafted as condemned stock and mutation mass,
itching to pierce the shape-shifters on a night
of tribunals in flash drives. Sequences of toxic
side-effects coaxed from pricked licks and one
octave chants, court triumphalists to mockup
and bulk. Eddy Daemon sashays his effete bod
against the press and the bleak community who
seek his agony as black-purple lump strangled
beside a hacked-off head. They're spoilsports
of an ancient peoplehood. We're the bystanders.
Eddy's the falsely accused executioner's heir.

Nebuchadnezzar 587

Fatigued with indolence, blunted by a clichéd
mesmerism—haggard, stony, half-buried wreck
and autoclave of ambition, Eddy Daemon sports
a gigantic horn of spite and ushers in a minute
era of hyphenation and circumventing sleights:
nerve-gleamed, raw-seamed, witty-sullen-jowled,
ghost-crabbed, thorn-tattered, messiah-hived-sick,
god-castrated, sod-smutted, swivel-jerked and tasty
morseled feminazi as manbearpig in low mondaze.
How unjubilant and malice-yielded! Nothing stays
the course, gloss-throated and flaked in foaming
at the mouth. Cylinders and spires pass from sight.
There's no chance to get a bearing. Even to scroll
back to Ezra's Walt concession stigmatizes clarity.

Creation 32

Solemnly meshed white to a fizzle against fuses,
the clenched fist of a chosen rant sealed up like
ambergris, disintegrates in an opal powder damp
with the acid residue of invisible ink. Eddy scraps
the monolith with its synoptic slab of punctured
wrists and skinned anatomical snuff boxes. Snorts
some snuff, the jolted god-coded brand with kick
and spring-loaded variety: piquant (crown), floral
(wisdom), mentholated (understanding), bordeaux
kindness), apricot (severity), plum (beauty), cola
(eternity), camphor (splendor), rose (foundation),
kingship (bourbon), plus twenty-two Adam-named
nostrils made of rosewood to round out the binding
clause to scrap. He feels unborn in choiring wings.

Lodge 99

Yoking the frieze of its parabola and rosaries,
the elect see Eddy motion the Mongol's *tengri*
with a lariat to cluster a *hadith*: a pitchblende
rescuing the *Most High* from tatterdemalions.
The belched words loaf. Eddy tweets: "a sweet
zombie Jesus zipperhead cocks a procreant urge,"
from a hyperactive account. The elect become
a flashmob and gangrape a bronze mascot. Eddy
admires his whatchamacallits and zomviruses,
admires himself as throwback or new coming
in the postseason with fireworks. Overriding
is impossible. It's a rerun of a cable program
called *Night of Lodge 99* filmed in Reykjavík,
Iceland. Eddy sneers. We have betrayed him.

Stonehenge 108

Eddy's daguerreotype nostalgia is a mental
health issue or *harshad* number in the golden
ratio. He dated a cow-herd *gopi* named Ms.
Uptard and called her his *far-swooping elbow*.
To undress her in *billowy drowse* and unclasp
her *japa* beads is to fall away as nirvanic cliché
of neodruidic gongs of revolt, devolving in red
infradimensions. Is saren stone red? Mr. Daemon
says it is, like a red marauder. A silica marauder
of silicified sandstone? Only to piss off the nasty
ultraforge trolling youtube to bully. Eddy's lintels
are held in place with mortise and tenon joints.
On October 8th, Eddy will propose to Ms. Uptard.
She'll be *umadbro*. His cravat will be a slipnoose.

Helix 144

Eddy sucks on dormant strands of red junk-gum
dispatched as the drenched spur of *Everpresence*.
It's raining in *The Land of Nucleic*: raining imps
and fat trolls. Eddy sees his dim past reversed
as salver and complains bitterly to the manager
of the field office. It turns out that the junk-gum
is human flesh and Eddy's a smoker: a *lymtudor*
whose femur turned into melted cheddar cheese.
It also turns out that the manager isn't Mr. Henry
Ham but rather Dr. Henry Ham, a jurist famed
for patenting red junk-gum. Eddy chomps, spits
and cries out "Vibila 144, Psalm 144, Sonnet 144,
144 Mahjong tiles and this goddamn Section 144
of the Bangladesh Code of Criminal Procedure."

Anthropoid 3761

It all comes down to the prophesied sedge:
achenes and solid stems, the blackthorned scag
skullcap and skinsuit of woody lobes with spikelets.
In the marsh, the worn down nub of *concupiscent
curds* ribs the mascaraed bugger, one or another
as plunger-name of the raw crease. Today, Eddy's
nosed, clutching his sachet of cosmetics in his gold
clipped komodo-dragon bag. No nostalgia. No edits.
No quiddity with its affected monism. It's the last
season of day one. We're on our way *kthxbai*! Omg
liek u wana c my fab nu jurnal? Dude, no, you make
me sick n00b. Something about searing sophistry
and prelapsarian catpiss. Incomplete, bottomline.
Eddy prostrates before the doorjamb in defeat.

Metron 6000

In the *logoi* of opposition, pick tragic *anceps*
like sub, ti, un, neg, haz, cide, mur, par, des, crit
to displace the choked genre. Eddy Daemon did.
The botched Eddy Daemon, belly-blooded usurper
of mythopoeic zones tagged zero-day flaws. Rename
him Eddy Mêlée, but it's an empty threat. Nothing
but a white room with a brown metal folding chair.
No Jabbok River, just faucet water in a plastic cup.
Not belly-blooded, the blood-brain barrier's endfeet
have been crossed. The condemned stock? The age
of the messiah is a farce. The rank and file have lost
their nerves bloated with endgame. At least Eddy's
here, Z:Lined in the stalled sever, but still here
as Henry Daemon without bats, bored by aliases.

Subatomic 13.798

Grand malpractice, defamation of character, vitriol,
slander and dealings in all things despoiled: *ermahgerd
mah fravrit berks*, says Eddy as a drogen-decreated
version of himself. He fears the vice versa of a lost
tribe of gas, demurs into baryonic dark matter as Eddy
Hubble, the extheist of crusty halos. To Eddy's credit,
active brain-spoors of word-spill course in their sap.
What about prior to? Eddy imagines a heavy residue
of curvy onion booty. How did cosmology become
garbaged with the wild scent of soft porn? Spin fast
forward to a galactic bulge threshing an apology:
his nuptials were clusters. He affected the outcome.
The topos is in the billions. Eddy rides the carrousel
at 2 pm on Thursday redisposing the verdict of bang.

Mandelbrot 3.14159

Self-belabored, crushed, mislead, overreached,
upgathered and glitched, Eddy auditions for lead
role in *Eddy Benoit, Fractal King of Carpathia*. He
claims descent from the Hyksos, postures and acts:
*I have no spur/to prick the sides of my intent,/but
Only vaulting ambition, which o'erleaps itself/and
falls on the other*. A bucket falls from the catwalk,
hits Eddy in the head. He passes out in a lit muck
of oils and hacked-off heads. A blue-red cardioid
and period bulb attracts cycles of three fixed points
in x-flux. Eddy vies for fantasist in this bad prequel.
He concedes to join the *xjokerz*, lying on his back
in the psych ward. He begins to count the *p/q-limb*,
yields to π, Q-tipping the mad bytches of his sad lot.

Tenebrae $A^2 + B^2 = C^2$

In the *penal colony* of the *wanky* literati, the black
hearse of iconostasis drips creamy wax on a virgin's
thighs. Eddy redacts, is bout to put a *thizz* in his gut,
spark a *bleezy* and take it from there *yadadamean*?
The hooded revert to the Law of Cosines. Atchoos
and a few belches later and the *Kingdom of Heaven*
appears in fumes of kryptonite. Eddy hums *leçons
de ténèbres*, logs in to LinkedIn as Pastor Sébastien
Gaudelus to perfect the transubstantiation of angels
and endorse a colleague. Time to brush the *fauxhawk*
gnarled with dyed streaks. Time to stoke good news
hate with n-dimensional chants, proving the saved
are saved and acing their *introdouches*. Eddy slips
away, sandaled in sackcloth like a rogue *clinamen*.

Zoas 4

Eddy boasts that his four volumetrics of etcetera
are valencies of carbon, confusing darker matter
with rants about beryllium's steel-grey gas sheen
as syncretic link to Albion and this *quijibo* named
Irma Vala. Eddy unloads his druidic penny stocks
where mendicant and margrave stage phony wars
with the leg bones of Tasmanian Devils. *Textholes*
back Irma Vala, demand net neutrality or a hack.
Too bad Irma's a *twink*. Eddy once styled himself
as a bit of an unengraved rogue in *leetspeak*. Now,
Eddy's a soap-bubble in a bathtub frieze. He feeds
carrots to his beagle Northrop Frye. Deism is born,
unfinished as *traffic tetris*. Eddy reenters the agon
of a first folio, but none survived the prison break.

Liber 777

The *magick* of penta, slick and lethal, red-gaudy
and libertine, in bedlam with posse, foredoomed
as if *queefing* Lou Andreas-Salomé with *The Ars
Goetia*. Eddy recites lines from *The Black Pullet
Grimoire*, refreshing his necromancy and spank
bank. He waves a black flag with a skull, screams
ignant ass-bitch at Heauton Timoroumenos who
smotes a rock in Horeb with a laudanum drip.
Initiates are baptized in crystal quicksand, wear
satin shoes, *challax* with a mattress *clapstain*
named Lady Naiad. Venusian incense burns.
Miasma spurts. Naiad's *vajazzling* for added
bling effect. Eddy grins like Nosferatu, blows
a kiss to his legions who are all eroto-comatose.

Lemma $2^{32} \approx 4\times10^9$

Coagulants of battery cells cocked in terra cotta.
Eddy's *obscurum,* hive-spoiled, not consigned,
is cauterized with tokens and garlands of ibids.
He's on a trek of fell-sides *alt-tabbin'* to deflect
grit as the assclown of a thorny smear campaign.
His graffiti of alien hatred with red-ant queens
and fuzzy tongues, pelts hailstones in a mesh
of seed-ice and a gang cache of rusted bullets.
Eddy's brain-bleaching again with acid splits.
Now what? Eddy's tries to catch a *chapqueef*
schlicking his *chode.* Brain-bleaching is fun,
especially when *cornbeefashtaging* as canon
with a cutting edge morphology like this one.
His privacy's harsh. His accountability, zero.

Gross 15.89

Eddy's sector output roughs obese, ripsaw bronze.
He pukes in the colonnade with staves, a cupidon's
grimace as durable goods like *laquearia*, stealing
the *shakespeherian rag*. He mocks Albert Eliot's
supply side economics of fire sermons, that cliché
of unreal cities littered with gashouses. Carthage
stinks, that's why the market's mudcracked, limp
and imputed. Eddy refuses to understand *shantih*
and the debt ceiling, back to his codependences
on Dr. Hieronymo and Madame Sosostris' manic
pills. He gets the names wrong, deters a beating
and an obit in the consumer price index, wearing
slippers and a camisole reading *The Wall Street
Journal* like a magnus martyr of exchange rates.

Kairos 1307

Eddy returns from slaughter as a rogue Templar
sporting bloody tonsure, mantels and a red cross,
first shouting *Omne Datum Optimum* on a black
warhorse, then screaming *dieu n'est pas content,
nous avons des ennemis de la foi dans le Royaume.*
Papal bull of burnt calves, thighs and hands, torso
and forearms, breasts, upper chest and face. Eddy
makes a grid of rods which are placed on forked
sticks, then ties the victims to the stake, lit by fire
underneath, so that little by little, Eddy's acolytes
scream in torment. Toralis Prae du Philip, dubbed
Eddy's heraldic double, takes three hours to die,
the slow grip of a rope to a neck through spiked
iron rings. Milky cross phlegm is idolatry in Paris.

Curlicue $x^2 + 3x - 4 = (x + 4)(x - 1) = 0$

Eddy's digital cartouche or Giorgio Vasari's Tuscany
self-portrait? The 1765 *de l'Isle globe*? An epiphany
in Tyska Skolgränd or Franz Anton Bustelli's *Pair
of lovers* in Nymphenburg porcelain? That sexed
mineral mullite raw with feldspar, ball clay, glass,
bone ash, steatite, quartz, petuntse and alabaster:
orgy in a kiln, fired fine to one zero and four x's,
prone to malware uploaded from a sick spambot
named hermes/waloraweb052/b2330 equals zero,
when x squared preempts the curlicue. It's said.
Endtime as Little Lord Fauntleroy's hair braids
on Eurt Nobain. Is Eddy still here? He yells rebel
and strings together coil, curl, gyre, ringlet, roll,
scroll and whorl, fatally wounding his squiggles.

Cosmographicum 1596

Johannes "Eddy Daemon" Kepler's catastrophic myth
of a rogue monk named Dr. Milton Polyhedra, died
in the Eggenberg Palace in Graz surrounded by petrel
and porpoise. He was buried below the *alte galerie*
with a chandelier, faïence stove, monochrome silk
damask wall covering and sconce. How about some
vexed bafflement? Hans Ulrich von Eggenberg's life
isn't unenvied with white gloves. Again, the salvages
are dry and anti-mimetic. How about that strict counter
reformatory policy? Unlock the linear year and the three
laws of orbital dynamics usher in perfect unity as hush
of blue holiness. Our loyalty is a common oath: you
and the unnamer. We should be so lucky to gnostically
brood, free of anxiety, not there yet and sauntering.

Degree 6

Eddy pledges a curse, his body a reflex splay of glut
with spillage for the oppressed and upgathered. Tell
it to Defroc Maestro, subliving off the unself-remitted
spoils of repeat. It's a grudge, really, unassuaged, aped
with oxygen boils. Failed actors from Theatre Spambot
loiter in code with scalpels. Add a corpse, blood-mote
with liquefied red-black scent of bile and crusty thresh,
and voila, Eddy's brain's an impostume. Then, vertex
sets revert to the pseudo-random, between lemma, node
and hyperedges. The disproportionate nod of appeal
has somethinx to do with it, but Eddy's empathy pales
in comparison to his dispeopled fraud. Natwarking op
to unsnap the coaxial medulla to meet Defroc Maestro
in the crawlspace above the high false ceiling and beg.

Digamma 13:17-18

Straightening as blades of a millicrystal, the porous,
lumpy clump soils the mix in the beard of patriarchs:
a mix of charred hands, almonds, whirring cudgels
and ghetto rose petals bedevil the devil with rubia
prayer thongs. How many shades of red? Crimson, red
ruby, scarlet, ochre, dyed silk and Chinese lacquerware,
burgundy and vexilloid red, strained in carmine. Eddy's
pissed red, download's Mark Rothko's *Four Darks in Red*
before flinging his laptop out the window. His complaints
are vast: red winds cut his throat, delegitimizers bloody
Saturn, invective reddens with rust, and those friggin
ancillaries courting nocturnal emissions. Revelations
are pranks, beast-sure, leaking classifieds with lunch
orders. Face it, Eddy's a malcontent in a red chair.

Embedded $n \leq m(m+1)(3m+11)/2 f: M \to R^n$

Game theory on an onyx tabletop made for Orpheus,
half-hacked in the mud, somewhere courts coevals
and the orphic daemon: vindicates the cracked dome,
minus the pulp and obliquity tutorials, among zipper
heads, never ceased to exist nor muffle incipit clanks
as secrets are the formaldehyde of a slice mind. Eddy
self-selects to self-correct, gray-violet, emblazoned
on a stolen t-shirt, points to garbage, sperm, lead-lined
balloons and distilled quotients in the form of crocuses.
Haphazardary is a chronistic Madame on three stumps.
Tomes blaze with couriers and hostile ones, fish-packs.
In pukings of assent. Something concrete approaches,
swerves away, exploding brains with a car bomb. No
rsvp. In this theory, one size fits all the naked Satans.

Vecextract $(7m\lambda)(9m + 2.87\lambda - 13m \equiv -\lambda \bmod(2m - 2\lambda)$

Eddy's an infisted impresario decked with a new brutalism, charms the scene with a megaphone, malachite frisbees, platinum axe, hydrangea spoons, pleated muslin and convex speculum. There is no way out of portraiture, not even ping, pathos, reptile eggs nor the mangod defaulted tributaries suppressed in mockery, blaming himself. One of these sets will be exotic, duly sliced and garnished with condiments of resolve. Formulaic will cripple his advances and stammer. To what infinity belongs the first aid kit? There's a reliquary to keep a bargain, the payouts. It's complicated. It doesn't matter if *de imagine mundi* threatened his livelihood. Circa 2013 at the extreme point of legibility, that's where privacy stakes its claim, and Eddy's released from his lease. Sum up! Elastic fetters hedge the bigger stakeholders with barb wire.

Scalar 299,792,458

Usurped by the imposter and rejecting sacraments, Eddy
perfects the idea of a degraded origin and contracts self
limitation into the divine breathing-in of red cataclysm.
He shucks off anthropoids, godmen and the primordial
imps of ruin, fearing futurity. At stake, sick catastrophes
gnawing at transmission with the jaws of hominids. He
shams the role with a descensus of impersonality waxing
creation's first violent tropes: contraction and withdrawal.
Why does Eddy fail to emanate? Is it due to casting-out?
The imposter says Eddy's mocking Elohim, wretchedly
sabotaging devotion to fake catastrophe creation myths.
What's trending? The broken occupy their belatedness.
Whose belatedness? Multiple choice: a) Eddy Kadmon
b) Eddy Valentinus c) Eddy Luria d) Phenylketonurics.

Rewritecond //:http%2://%{HTTP_HOST}[R=301]

Eddy's avatar is DDoS, beast of sick overload. Notice
the trigger errors in the microcode of the machine. It's
all in the thrashing and resource starvation: forge, spoof,
smurf and the proverbial ping of death unleash biatches
of malware. Today's a la carte menu features the SYN
flood, Teardrop attack, Peer-to-peer attack, Nuke attack,
OWASP HTTP Post Denial Tools and the ever spicy
R-U-Dead-Yet? Eddy floods the bandwidth, rememes
DDoS, GDoS, the microaggression rebooted cleanse
with a theurgical gassing. This is Eddy's respoofed
packet of derailment, his avatar gone viral as ripped
off *Theater of Cruelty* busting up firewalls and BSBs
synproxies. Face it, Eddy cops a grin, his godhead
has an ISP hagiography of saint-zippered droidals.

Cipher 0

Zierorəʊ, ziroʊ, nɔt, nil, zilch, zip, zéro, zefiro, safira, sifr, ifrfr, śūnya, zephyrus, nada, goose egg or duck egg and scratch or love in two slanted wedges subtracted from three hooks and divided by zero—the small circle with a long overbar zero—Hellenistic or Venetian then morphed into Omicron to emerge as a glyph for the zero digit written in the shape of a dot. Eddy minus Eddy squared by an empty tortoise shell, uncounted in knotted cords, undoes historiography, biography, autobiography, memoire, belles letttres, travel guides and preemptive blurbs of praise, ebiled in ginormity and hashtags such as *#zxcvbnmasdfghjklqwertyuiop, #zwix,* hearing zombies stuttering on z-words. He is Eddy $1/-0 = -\infty$ and $1/+0 = +\infty$ that he is Eddy, less undefined for $\pm0/\pm0$ and $\pm\infty/\pm\infty$, either/or $x \rightarrow 0^-$, $x \rightarrow 0-$, or $x \rightarrow \uparrow 0 \ddot{Y}$ Daemon.

Scatotheological 1

Eddy Antoine Marie Joseph Daemon died of an overdose
of chloral hydrate in 1948 at the age of 51. The bastards
Mickey Finned him with chemical reagents: the bastards
of psychosis that are in Rodez in the Aveyron department,
haunted by the Visigoths and Franks. Add neuralgia, bouts
of severe depression, meningitis and addiction to opium,
laudanum, Tarahumaran peyote and uncut Afghani heroin,
and *Pour en Finir avec le Jugement de dieu* deploys alarming
cries, screams, grunts, onomatopoeia and glossolalia over
a peoplescape of sadistic voyeurs. He called them bourgeois.
Is Eddy avatar, alias, identity thief, stand in, bodysnatcher
or lunatic of a counter-force? Fecal matter is a humor stuck
between the choleric and melancholic. He gestured to prick
the divine arse, on March 4, now International Bowel Day.

Helix 2

In molecular daemonology, Eddy Daemon plus Eddy Daemon
doesn't equal a *Huffy Henry* polymer. At core, yet unswerved,
to work concurrently with *topoisomerases*, this Eddy jaunt
begins to improve the purity of his rapture. The phosphorus,
gleams, chinks and sweeps bend like green worn chains back
before the turning back of the impoverished unity. Dr. Sergey
Petoukhov's seminal book, *Biperiodical Table of Genetic Code
and a Number of Protons* has nothing to do with Eddy's "Helix
2." Fibonacci numbers and genetic codes are incidentally Eddy,
but not by definition. Eddy sulks. Henry sulked, once capturing
that grave Siamese face which, falling backwards, was ghastly
and boring. Who coined "headachy?" It was Achilles eating
chicken páprika, fainting with interest as all good clichés do.
Aren't there laws against this? Eddy traipses. He even struts.

Invokevirtual #16; //ethod java/io/PrintStream.println:(I)V

Nvokes an interface ethod on object *objectref*, whereas interface ethod is identified by ethod reference *index* in constant poolix (*indeddyxbyteI* << 8 + *indeddyxbyte2*) and *count* is the number of arguments to pop from the stack frame including the object on which the ethod is the sabprimd Eddy Daemon or greater than or equal to 1 jump to subroutine at *branchoffset* (signed int deconstrax ursigned bytes *branchbyteI* << 24 + *branchbyte2* < 16 + *brdaemonnchbyte3* < 8 + *branchbyte4*) and the return address on the stack pushes a constant *#index* from a constant pool (string, int, float or class type) onto the stack (wide *index* to deconstrax as *indexbyteI* << 8 + *ideddyxbyte2*) ext *opcode*, where *opcode* is either iload, fload, aload, lload, dload, istore, fstore, astore, lstore, dstore, or ret, to assume the *index* is 16 bit; or execute minc, when the *index* is 16 bits of a bagouted E.bot.

Apeiros $-\pi/2 \leq y < 0$ or $0 < y \leq \pi/2 \sum a_n \infty$

Calqued from a pastiche which is actually a pâté of squab forcemeat with cepes, anise and combava jus, Eddy kicks Zeno of Elea in the mouth and is expelled from The Eleatic School: all that is immeasurably subtle and profound is gat to Eddy. Pherecydes of Syros, the *Enûma Eliš,* the Rig Vedic *Hiraṇyagarbha*, Hesiod nor Anaximander matter. The *arché* is neither eternal nor ageless. In fact, the *arché* is uhere, Mr. Arché and he's 82 and delusional. Rumor has it that Mr. Arché is Eddy Daemon's father. Out of his vague and limitless body, sprang a central mass. This is a non sequitur. The blazing orb is a farce ordained by revolt and disappointment. No progeny, rather the theft of a macabre mouse named Mrs. Eunomia. Attendance at the wedding of Mr. Arché and Mrs. Eunomia was poor. The royal houses didn't merge. Eddy is a bastard.

Promethazine 00603-1585-58

Eddy is a roleptic medicate, comprised of (RS)-N, N-methyl-1-(10H-pheno-thiazin-10-yl) propan-2-amine, tagged a teaspoon of 10mg's of Codeine: 6.25mg's of Phosphate 7% as soupy pink Promethazine Hydrochloride. Eddy Lucifer today, he undead, postnarcotic nausea, paranoid wash of opioids. It's not a mere conjecture spawned from months of reclusivity. It's one alias to add to the mix with isomers, esters, ethers, salts, popcocas leaves and ecgonine. Are these recessives aliases? Hey, recede into usury were the real Eddy Daemon is a raptured narcotic? Ask'em a Greek physician Galen of Pergamon. Doctor Galen, or may I call you Aelius (tapun intended), or Claudius, is we duped by Eddy's silent partner, the infernal sexpot Sig Mund? Galen is the son of Aelius Sigmund. He died in 99 CE, in 17 CE. His *Du Motu Cordis* was attributed to Eddion of Daemonica.

Sertraline 68180-0352-02

Falsely accused say as Shylock, Hester Prynne, Jean Valjean, Quasimodo, Lennie Small, Frankenstein's Monster, Severus Snape or Carrie White, Eddy's a bedlamite addicted to (1S,4S) 4-(3,4-*dichlorophenyl*)-N-methyl-1,2,3,-*tetrahydronaphthalen* 1-amine, or less blurry, Sertraline. Its chemistry as developed from the godbrain. Basted by a horriforic revision of chemist Reinhard Sarges, Eddy's godbrain is אֱלֹהִים צֶלֶם, (*Zelem Eloh*), *Imago Dei*, leading us to a self-fulfilling outer intprophecy: Eddy D and God D are afflicted by major diprezzion, body dysmorphic, obsessive compulsive disorder, premenstrual dysphoric, premature ejaculation and posttraumatic stress disorder. Doirony and report a shared incarnadine of a pink, fleshy nubmidy French *incarnadin*, or from the Old Italian *incarnadino*, nixed by a Latin *incarnates*, first used in 1605.

Clarithromycin 68382-0762-14

Eddy Binoclar, Eddy Bioclar, Eddy Biaxin, Eddy Crix,
Eddy Clarihexal, Eddy Clacid, Eddy Claritt, Eddy Clac,
Eddy Clarac, Eddy Clariwin, Eddy Claripen, Eddy Clar,
Eddy Claridar, Eddy Fromilid, Eddy Infex, Eddy Klaric,
Eddy Klacid, Eddy Klaram, Eddy Klabax, Eddy Monoc,
Eddy Resclar, Eddy Baxy, Eddy Truclar and Eddy Vikro,
have all been subpoenaed by Lord Archibald Lux Loopy
Ototoxicity to die by lethal inject dis myoneural junction
the High Council. Defamation of character as tort of libel
won't defray their stay of execution. Her'em cuse of mass
murder with tropes of hydrogen cyanide and misprision.
Ototoxicity will administer the injections of pentobarbital,
pancuronium bromide and potassium chloride. Oto Lord
has dythsma. He straps the Eddys to green, vinyl gurneys.

Apocalypse 5775

Eddy "Skyquake" Daemon shot a ginger midget named Hat
Shuah with a Yesu assault rifle below a sculpture of a silver
ceramic tower heater. It's model number 5775 with a giant
auto-off coming of the *moshiach* timer. For the sake of clarity:
ἀποκάλυψις or *apocálypsis*, from ἀπό and καλύπτω meaning
uncovering, nuanced for endtime and redeemed in the rebirth
of Adam. Rumor had it that Hat had been a metempychotic
Adam. Skyquake was no preterist. Hat had to be taken out.
Gesundheit Mister Eusebius and Mister Chrysostom. Tonight,
Daniel 12:2: *"Multitudes who sleep in the dust of the earth will
awake: some to everlasting life, others to shame and everlasting
contempt."* Ampersand: this pulpy fiction stings those who say
that Eddy "Skyquake" Daemon is a cheap Jules Winnfield.
The date's a palindrome. The next one's in a hundred years.

Omen 1973

Eddy Daemon doesn't tolerate portraiture, autopsy or inquest.
He favors the soul's internment and savage mimicry, but not
at the expense of the brute epigone of Samael's seed. How's
das unheimliche, Eddy? Haven't we seen you in *Omen I, II*
and *III* as Damien Thorn augmenting Cassiopeia? Are those
the seven daggers of Megiddo in your bag? It's time to reify
the Star of Bethlehem. Weren't you made redundant, or fired
by the CDC? Both: insect-armed, snub-tailed, creep-crawled
with 666 burnt on your scalp, you, the beast's acolyte which
translates as to reckon. An Aramaic *Sitrah Ahra* to Arethas
of Caesarea's seven names: *Lampetis* (lustrous), *O Niketes*
(victor), *Teitan Palai Baskanos* (sorcerer), *Kakos Odegos*
(bad guide), *Alethes Blaberos* (harmful), and *Amnos Adikos*
(unjust lamb). Daemons are orgasmic in raptures of selfies.

Antipersonnel 1,200–1,310 ft/s (370–400 m/s)

Eddy "Dysphoria" Daemon is clinically unsound, Freud's
family romance notwithstanding. He sports a cleaved toupee,
horned eczema, and a hacked-off face with scabs. Charm
is blood in him as he monopolizes social settings. His wit,
embossed with a *pas-de-deux*, admits fingered *différance*
and obscurity. It's a quaint scatotheological hoax to occupy
and emit scented gaiety on his hosts. He's a surly, sly, coy
and crude socialite stuck in a *mise-en-scène* with a hussy
named Elizabeta Borderline. It's all applauded rancor, flash
mouthed malice and petty duress. His timely suicide steals
reincarnation: pile-voltaged, gleam-surged, drab-jacked,
dumb-struck in a pit of phosphorescent gods ratifying plots.
His funeral is a media event. The Mothers of Satan speak
of acetone peroxide, detonating their M57 claymore vests.

Cheirokmeta 300

Silence is cooked like gold, says Eddy, in a grand theft
of chemistry, metallurgy, physics, medicine, astrology,
semiotics, mysticism, spiritualism, and art. It is hermetic
and syncretic and reminds us of such maggids as Hermes
Trismegistus, Roger Bacon, Saint Thomas Aquinas, Tycho
Brahe, Thomas Browne, Parmigianino, Albertus Magnus,
Agrippa, Paracelsus and Jakob Böhme. Eddys sulks before
The Philosopher's Stone, knowing that his rather tumescent
intentions to advance the actuarial worth of a sibylline oracle
will result in the use of spagyrics as feline amour. Alchemy
is blight against a backdrop of inertia and fading *gloriole
nimbus* with coterie of frizzed sirens. Here he is again then,
posthuman, in the obscure soteriology of a moral nebulae
with pure carat and an arsenal of stolen *unctuous platitudes.*

Nazarene 33

The *secernere* splits from the consignation of shrouds, keeper
of surplus bile and the legacy of the eschaton and redeemer
of a priestly sect who will rule *The Holy Land*. The dead
will rise. Graves will open. Ashes will reconstitute covenants
of bone, flesh and limb. Those morphed between paleontology
and cybernetics, will return to the streets. Not the recent dead,
nor the ignobly dead such as lumpen martyrs and scholars,
but all human forms from hominids to spambots with organs.
This is barely it. The return of the repressed will gut archives
and accrue *archontic* power to chafe against their internetic
hedge. Notice their beady-eyed lechery, poisons, fissures,
gaps, and amnesiac forgetfulness. Eddy will be skinned,
hanged, quartered and disemboweled. His salted and severed
head will be attached to the top of a Bedouin's walking stick.

Hacker 1389

Phrenologists as spambots named Slurpee Eddies, infect
the internet with the Crusading Enpap-X virus. Bad News.
Eddy's brain is clogged with purple codeine phosphate,
a double cheeseburger, eidolons and fealties of *fort-da*.
He represses Pauline dread and reclaims *Eretz Israel*
from the Aleppo Mamluks 1389 capture of Jerusalem.
Not Jerusalem, the Levant, beating back the Mongols
at the *Battle of Ain Jalut*. It's a Slurpee Eddies thing.
The problem doesn't lie with a cabal of killing gods,
but in the ingenuity they possess returning amorphic
matter to physical form. Eddy yearns to shapeshift
to catch a commuter train to the Temple Mount.
No megalomaniacs here stalking Facebook photos.
This is at last Eddy's shibboleth. He writes code.

Panegyric 1844

Holy, Holy, Holy is the selective serotonin reuptake
inhibitor in pale-blue with anachronistic hints of Joseph
Pancoast's 1844 essay on the advantages of bloodletting
in "A Treatise on Operative Surgery." Hail dopamine
and serotonin. Eddy says, pay it forward, upside down.
Ibid. He demands fearful symmetry, routine blunt
verities, but not a theater, nor outdated *desuetude*
of fatal chains. Then, it's Happy Hour. The menu:
shots of Sierra Silver Tequila, Bacardi 151, Devil's
Springs Vodka and the 190 proof Everclear Vodka.
Here's a toast to suburby agitpropists, the nonplussed
with their zeitgeist of anticoncenci consensus. Eddy
fancies a recoil from the undefined way to the latrine.
He's the soul-jacker of an extinction blood gang.

Dow 16,544.10>115.15 (0.69%)

The spoof DJ indices, minus liability, self-insured, gives net
debt equaltoless than actuarial death. Eddy's donor advised.
His property risk conjoins a tax benefit asto *a prioir* models,
typically hedged with an assumption of *ceteris paribu,* prior
to Keynesian proofs of gains and probate. Liquidate Eddy,
say the stockholders, falsify the input-output as labor-value
remnant of over-price, dealt on the inside, then zero-sum.
Abscond donors, stigmata of a spent rolodex. To steward
is to usurp the ethic of the godfather. Kvetch on Facebook
his malady of the upskirt. Yes, upskirt the puberty of sum,
this individual gift of a million dollars. Virginity is crossed.
We're in the database and have legacy. *Homo economicus,*
launch the billionaire Eddy, greater than prior amalgams,
in algorithms, in initial public offering, splitting stocks.

Suicidium 801

Suicide, from *sui caedere* among philologists. Eddy Daemon
waxes Rodin's *The Thinker*, thin now on punctuos sasitudes.
Whip a stiff hanging or saunter to the country for a pesticide
poisoning pastoral. There's some organochlorine, straight up.
Lest we forget the proverbial firearm. Self-immolation tagged
as a confession grope. Eddys tags a selfie. *When a problem
comes around you must whip it*, but Eddy's a gimpy social
phenom of one disviewing the epistemology of a suicidal
ideation. Rodin's not our waxed, it's Edvard Munch's *Skrik*.
Generalized Anxiety Disorder (GAD) or gadfly? Not panic,
Dr. Daemon, the new discovery is not equalizing. It's canon
envy as gluten-free diet. Eddy opts for evolutionary mismatch.
N-touch. N-pain. His amygdala wants the sensory data to end.
The death of gray matter, e.killjar by depoison cup of coffee.

Tongva 1542

Eddy trespasses on Mrs. James Rosemeyre's (*née* Narcisa Higuera) land, some 4,000 square miles manifested in the destiny of bolted Europeanization. Only the most powerful get to be birthed as *née,* their *Uto-Aztecan* blood a favorite among reclining tourists attracted to sedentary palms. Don't dis the *Hokan* with *xwak* as *Proto-Yuman* pronounced ko:kx. Nothing dwindles as effect of drought. Migrants pushed the region. Not our weak, belly *polis* with crass connotations. The exploration occurred in 1542. Spazmoids of forced derelocation, and Eddy wonders. Bad Eddy. Diseases of rapid collapse. I, Eddy's, rapid relapse. Yours, when ceded. *Endonym's* were recorded. 1903 is later than 1542. A *Tongva* woman named Juana Maria was the last surviving speaker of *Nicoleño.* Juana was Eddy's first wife. She died in 1853, which doesn't help our historicity of Eddy's efforts to hide his gene pool. Nothing rhymes with Orange, except scaled mélange

Vodka 0.121

Not Noah's intoxi/gimp of romanticized Michelangelo, but Eddy's fermented potatoes. Blood in units of mass: вод- (*vod-*), ild euphoria, postfix water: *gorzałka*, twiced Cyrillic, grainy to highs of dripnose with sorghum—Eddy Molasses. Say it. Eddy Sugar Beet. Foreshots of heads and tails. Ethyl acetate lip gloss tagged by the glass. Toss back the fusel oils, for we/wo the Eddy strippers of rectified spirits. *Disequilibrium* poses for death with its buddy *nystagmus*. Back at the arse creek, red pepper and ginger vie for bison grass. Mutated krupnik, honeys the nalewka, to merely poke the tincture, made by maceration and confused by a false friend cognate. Seal it. Ferment it. Suck the chilly-bone stem. Eddy tilts toward analogues for one last time. Anise is a bitch in our bloodstream. Ours? What person? Eddy draws the line at barbaris, blackcurrant, cherry, green apple, lemon, vanilla and watermelon. Eddy's ultrapremium. He gags.

Reprise C/FF#9+D/GFSUS2/AB

Shimmy sham to bunt or yam through and thraut, bye-bye: no tell,
Eddy tells no one to waste this taste for free, yee against noture, yer
no telling, invents another music, in the case of a μ major, B natural
for an A natural in the right hand—boogaloo, formed in these usual
manners with one caveat, faux tension, when vatars shake it: booty
ust bandwidth to *Santa Ana Winds* without rain. Sister, this blood
of my brother shaking it, thumps a full concert, best in show: beats
and falls apart, but fades: Eddy's weak five o'clock shadow: dis Jung,
some yung man instead corrupts flesh as *nefesh* cleansing, not input
out, voicing of the second and third scale tone, keeps letter, text next
chord has its tonic on the 5th (A)—honey was that about say?, shame,
about me, last progeny—Rep died—Rep couldn't provide—he love,
he liar, pyre liar—Eddy, you sham—privacy, honored to be mong
worms, mong things—other, I left you uncoded: digits in redirects.

Monad ix

Segment and the name of a glyph's uber cliché: number one,
its own factotum as empty product, but instead with respect
to a unit, a serif at the top, traces roots to lines and originates
from similarity into a long upstroke, its case the perfect first
of the first person singular when prosody died. Eddy died later
in a separate symbol. It may be all decorative and confessional.
The function ix always equals i. Eddy's almost certain to occur:
his resin identification code, sorted among plastic, reprocessing.
Start the header. Backspace. He is a lighter element: hydrogen.
His divinity is Neoplatonic. With raw bliss, he burns Plotinus
because his first edition Porphyry was lost in the fire. God's
number? Only permitted among players who disappear later
in hedges. These savage curiosities when so much else seems
to matter. It's worth, literally, in human terms, in only one.

Écouté 1791

Misappraisal, these last ambles seen eyeless without praise,
to steal disguised as papier-mâché cunning—no crosshatch,
no *bas-relief* to order his bod: himself hopes until he submits,
at fifty-two, to ambling clefts of Eddy latched in self-stroking:
clings in not self-pitiless, yet a *truthiness*, craving the red sun.
Eddy's resentment (French pronunciation: *rəsãtima*), voiced
uvular fricative, social class marker retells Nietzsche's course
ressentiment as the charm of *sentir*. Who are Eddy's enemies?
His genius is maladaptive—tearhe apart in vapid god-hunger.
This offered as the quest of cyberterrorism. Took longer to die:
rex tremendae and the first eight bars of the *Lacrymosa*. Eddy's
Picardy third was ruled out for white noise. These red swells.
This common internment. This rash like millet seed: *hitziges
frieselfiebe* here for us frizzy-haired selfies as big data trolls.

Wunderkind 1962

Vodouisants, don't the latecomer this time, to the few still
as *sèvitè*, unknowable creator god (lower case "G"): human
affairs—*bon dieu*—*vodouists* direct their worship toward
spirits in this unironic state, down before, the fool, come
and get it—*gris-gris*, worn on Eddy, sublime in his gothic
ire to touch flesh without fingers—code this in your hands:
voodoo a doll, his pure *Amurkin* lexicon as patriotic as air.
Spangle, a hand on his heart: his ancestor's region, intact
in schisms of toxic roots for *figuier maudit* are many used
orthographies for this word: world, new epoch, new prefix
avoided by a certain sect of scholars. Eddy has no memory.
Eddy has no self-defense, exercised in dishonor and greed.
Pure Self Eddy! Kill this bastard from nineteen sixty-two!
Coolness is overvalued, designed silent as texted libation.

Denkstätte 1945

Dr. Eddy "Stacheldraht" Daemon triggers errors in this divine
alias: unstable lockup, thrashing in a constant state of paging,
pings death: peer-to-peer if ports are allowed or not, barbwires
in, client back onto the client's dialectic of enlightenment. Pat
the *Denkstätte* with gloved hands as it parades teardrop attacks
with neo-nonpitched Serialism. Stacheldraht hums the timbre
as he treks through the mysterium horrendum. Stop the syzygy!
How much more can be omitted? Two metrical feet as a single
unit, stirs even the polyglots. Tone slips into biopolitics. Eddy
is the oppressor. Dr. E. Stacheldraht Daemon is the oppressed.
We all hide it from the whole even in errors. Five seconds later,
Eddy is oppressed. Nothing here can comport. Nothing slouches.
We'll poke the zeitgeist. Please respond fulfills our antithetical
natures to kill a remote host, praying to ocasax of a cracked sun.

Modal 1961

Modal playing, mere vamps of two tonics, pedal points and drones:
the piece is built on *ottu*, or *ektar* or *dotara*, effects of a sustained
pitch: tags bouncier, rustic opening and trio section of a *scherzo*:
modal favors our favorite things: rank air of a lost individual: E
minor and E major, hypnotic—this cadenza, a dervish as Eddy
bridges to brood—upbeat's trill coda, freer but not as in any him:
waiting, waiting, waiting for die in the key of B♭: one octave, due
to the smaller bore of inflections Eddy can't cry: derived, scribed
in didn't trust himself nor plus flat-5th/sharp-4th, maybe a transfer
unless we alter the scale's blue note's tetrachord street Eddy A.
Modal lubricants, pomaded on sustains of amped, lick the death
itch of nostalgia—vamps it, tailgates it by piano *ostinato,* vamps
it again using scalar runs and solo *partitas.* His unmade bed's
sheets of sound is a death bed, *telos* of comfy rapture pillows.

Revelation 17:14–18

Fed neglecting the merged and blurred *ipede* of *vernate*:
Eddy's yoke-mate's a male alias of the *Whore of Babylon,*
seventh vial, purple and violet with seven heads and ten
horns of an afterclap. Simply put: Eddy's *alltheistic* yes,
no *bromances* other hard complexes instead—such things
as egotism, mental laziness, and sloppiness. *Degift* Eddy.
Hold the *Edict of Milan* in 313 responsible: love's *agape*
is his shibboleth, his *di voi pastor s'accorse il Vangelista.*
His easy, out-of-body shadow lives below his own level,
sinks back into unity, into *tenebrositas*—emptied form,
emptied shade, kicking back into closure, martyrs: *King
James* must continue a short space. A danger possesses.
Beast 7. Beast 17, among prime numbers, blood-drunk,
tongue-mashed, reigns over invisibles of Eddy's *uggos.*

Range 95-99%+

Esprit de corps is a surrogate key, the access port of a disfigured troll—*extortionate profit* desires a seigneurial to gain the talents of an *acq-hire* or say even an *acqui-hire* to prosper due startups. Will the *lixitae* of Orange County be speedier than these extreme herds? Heard of what? Herd of stocks. Nobody keeps up with *us to interpret.* Eddy has gadget fatigue. Eddy is vendor haste: grab. The canon has no genomes. No coding sequence names us now. New, untamed confessions wax era. It's urgent, yes. It's relevant. Nothing is more urgent, but will pass. Is Eddy Ezra? Ezra *beats noise to make terror.* How many *pediocres* publish? If history mattered? Eddy knows. We know Eddy's map maps a new writ in religion's county seat for civil pariahs. No one to end it don't. Nature and you don't matter, even as you extinguish these limits. Read yourself in Eddy's "not about me." Born to retell this alias.

Ubu 1896

Swap the canto stink for a realestate odor of *Père Cyber*:
ungodly anachronism of "kinging," when Ubu rips transport
with algorithms. The latest master race serves an immediate
need: Eddy can't get there. This mixed stealth of a sentinel
gene he lacks. A dear wife's overhead is in default. Children
he never tags, don't show up in the cult of these oppressed
likes of his admitted envoy. Today, no envoys, not even
a nuance demurs to place ceding pure was. Nothing was.
These chroniclers' find holders. Elegances find a crying.
No one lives in nothing done, especially Eddy as *Vale Tudo*.
Eddy's a lucky stiff with *jobie,* hatched from the least dark
eggs to forgive pardons critics spawn. How many critics?
They belong to the *School of Yaritza*. Eddy is denied entry
to King Turd's palace wearing the body of the dead bear.

Usher 1839

The failed lately of feeds and glueware's low mischief,
forfeit their tribune if rites failback under duress here
collapsing. It's the optic tract of a weak left eye's wide
slit of *amblyopia.* Hail the gripsack of ocular strength.
Is this like a satchel or a manbag? Declare the *fundus*
the audience, and hail the blur Eddy defocuses, a poke
of recall in the f/16 to f/32 range. Not these audiences,
those among the unconvinced performing in *The Fall
of the House Usher* who hear the thin crack. Eddy's
hyperesthesia is out of control today. His rosy cheeks
could say inter and may cause the tarn to glow blue.
Then, the zombie-cringe of a killbot's evil eye eyes
Eddy. He's renamed Edderick. His brain splits in two.
The blue crack widens eye-like twice beyond repair.

Decalogue 10

Eddy's *koine,* axed from the *lingua franca* of banned,
regards both cleansed of history and rumored to have
history, finally anachronistic—*Epistles* unsent in lieu
of his *lemonparty.* Don't dare to spin the bottle: femurs
turning into melted cheese wear a human lung as a hat.
To *lymtudor* is to smoke human flesh—Eddy smokes
his digi pepper jack, redacted from her healthy lungs.
Who her? She, the last one devoted to his sacred-empty.
Yell, hail instead: no, yell out *cephalapluering.* Heart
before the Priory of Daemon. Heart before the murmurs
of Eddy's autofiction. Heart, heart, heart to deca minus
one. Pick one: two graven or eight stealing T.S. Eliot's
theft. Coda—the Greek δέκα failsbetter as a kilogram
force, so outdated and romanticized as to be illegal.

Mali T624GPU

El dū yahwī ṣaba'ôt, or Eddy Daemon causes to be a host
of hash busters to hush jumbotrons, as obsolete as heavenly
armies. When did the High Priest in the Holy of Holies die?
Mercy-erased, hymn-skinned, rapture-wanked as a *hyperion
to a satyr* ruins the pure contempt of his love. Origins betray
the hosted exchange, hot buffers the *Kenite Exchange's* next
hop as packet hop and stele router gagging on lidded width.
Listen to pinpricks of the *Tetragrammaton's* arduity. Eddy
bleeds from the ears. Bad gaming *noob*-target for easy kills,
remembers memebers of the meme written on *Elephantine
Papyri* and recycled Mali-T624GPU as clichéd as hotshot
plagiarism. Perfect delivery: embed—*Yesha'yahu*—*Yahu*
saves the saved billions. If *illions* rise without b, compress
Eddy's *tetra, tri, di* and *hen* into vision or audition's joke.

Sequitur 2015

His subfield of colloids: foams, gels and the rarefied liquid
crystals of soft matter—such a common and neglected trait
of heartless rapture among layered goo. If he's hypnotized,
so are we in gloop, gook, gunk and glop's gummy muck
of sticky stuff. Eating gruel, burgoo and cawl with butter
and salt, connects bonds and polymer melts. Predictions
fail to motor the nerves of bubbles above his cartoon lips.
By contrast, rubber in tires, etc. He always overreaches
left in spite of enthalpic smiles—right in spite of a lipid's
found object. Eddy's internal degrees will never placate
the *not afraid* heroic us drawn across these test surfaces.
His passion segues to derive from the *passus* of billow.
Tilts to derive. Tilts to adagio with affix cum (= with),
by a string left standing to suffer ranked unholied non.

ISBN 978-0-9883713-4-7

Fine, shaken or tilted, subclass granular, finer in clumps
when flowing coarser except when wet as household dust
or powdered sugar—Eddy's top layer is a lunar *regolith*.
His *lithos* of the blank empty empties here *in situ*, sight
unseen and sight of the toner, applied to skin and tones
of gravel and sand. Eddy's bulk behavior causes cause
to clump like powder. Late and little inertia tend to go
with the flow, in nose and sinus, back to lungs to expel
him as miner's *phthisis*, or grinder's asthma or potter's
rot from chronic, simple *silicosis*. Eddy's a mudstone
of rare *argillite*, rarer *nuff* to burn acquisition's more:
more and more paste: more and more gel in a human
spine, way flowing freely is certainly way *au courant*.
His confession is a bio-angle of repose as fragile near.

Hyle $i^2 = -1$

Soma's ether of was is as Mr. Was said, Eddy's cleavage
of tongues is a sick *hydrostat*, works against him or a rad
cameo of *Prot* by a last guerilla theater in Proto-Germanic
hyle: wood and matter, not deed nor a jerk-lift caricature.
Hylomorphism only kills the *ousia*—just *morphē*, just ὕλη
skinned bare tonight, ending Eddy: the human ends Eddy's
gains and losses, body-soul prank inhabits the lying corpse
ceasing to be *nous*. Nothing rings like *hylomorphic* theory.
Eddy is fully body, makes up the body, itself after a death
to exist less than *not dark yet*, gives up these passive agents
for the simple Cartesian life, simply skinned not for body
but for univocity and impossible *haecceity*. Puzzlement
then distracts quiddity's stand against its subjective parts.
Three generations of murdered narratives lets no one go.

Fatale 69

Release starch to local mates whose 69 nanometres,
between the infrared, break middle clauses with red
kerosene lamps. Eddy lives in/on *bioluminescence*:
nobody's *chemiluminescence* reacts with his flask's
limited emission of heat. Confess, Eddy's a vibronic,
excited state of reactants imitating being our human
man, our being a human woman: *hominin clade* erect
in posture to fuck *australopithecine* or related *genera*.
Occupy extinct Eurasia. No one lives there, Ladytrix.
Did anyone really want a Ladytrix asbe of first fatale,
last womb? *Wīfmann* to *wīmmann* to *wumman* feely.
Eddy was always Eddie. Tag the Norman Conquest
when the labial changed to a man's *wambe* conquer.
Eddy's alchemy of copper bleeds Menarche's she.

Carthaginian 146

Eddy "Barbarossa" Daemon attempts to rule the sacrum's red
beard, waxing Herzog von Schwaben's first trip to the Eastern
region of Swabia: there, partnered with the multi-hyphenated
cisgendered, an old school Cisalpine Gaul, unmarks the norm.
When did he match their body/sex? In these seamless defenses,
in these *dictatorships of likes,* birthed accrued solely due to set
when born gifted. Other translump defeat more defeated sides,
sides subjugated simple and poised for a post-peace Eddy sex,
out-of-the-box and post-gendered genre. Carthage is conflict.
Carthage is finally heard, blinded by a cataracts of anecdotes.
Water starves motive. Eddy refuses to box glory. He humbles
bromide. He crazed with *craquelure.* He all but *Punic* risks.
He occupies the *cupi* of *womyn*-born *womyn: bych* of *ytches.*
Labels consider erasures, far, far ahead of the poultry smanx.

Chaetophobia 342

Hurlyburly's coiled s-curls balk a bobblehead spring
of jibber jabber. The magneto-follicle tilts back up
to goop, switched from papier-mâché to hot ceramic.
No prospect of belief, none but the nape's skin tone,
bored to death, neck wrung ezone slick with a glam
goldmine canned for greased up pomp. Unfix Eddy's
mane for a beat boy hairclip of combed hoochie koo.
About his red flared fringe, his Madame Majordomo,
as Eddy calls his hair, blow dry it with a vent brush
to add feathering to his hipster cred, his curl-cream
boho as coiffed side pricks of spurred casting gloss.
Avenge Eddy's pop pompadour in a redux of vellus
ughs, stroking neck-face lash back to the first bald
sénéchaux in training for the *chaetophobia* games.

Sonnetto 154

Hecatombs of Exter late in delu(Zion): Cathars, Druze, *Rose
Croix*—staccato half-sentences enter his flesh as Greek *Palin,*
or if palingenesis demurred to Vishnu's 10 in one carnations,
here in reach of Sonnetto's 154 embedded empties of an Orc.
Eddy's part fantasy race, part goblin, part crude *orqindi*: ogre
with pits for a frag-heart, broods to be born over again: reborn
as *swylce gigantas þa wið gode wunnon.* Eddy's mannish: see,
he's a *mannish boy*, a Neapolitan *orco* for empathy's cleanup.
Forgive Eddy for being human. He may have spread his proto
over a fit older than extant, bears pious nothing from nothing
in genius' progeny fading into blood. Yes, he sees the book
of the dead—the book of "Daddy" matters in adapted forms,
left ur-attended in the fulfillment of debt. Eddy's sons carry
his crucial *bardo*. Eddy's father died later. He lives farever.

Ratio 4:3

Eddy Parvenu betrays alterity—Eddy's ethnos surpasses
his dyad, his *theolatrous* impulses bent into *theomania,*
reveals his disclosive nature to count the tears of a wife.
Coiled in the crux, Eddy ungifts the heart's *via negativa.*
Es gibt, for now as hush of the tetralemic interpretation
of maya and pittance-paid dearth of ardor: Eddy decants
his wares on the midden of rapture, spells out potpourri
of bleak and waits for his wife. His wife, his global girth
to stay foreclosure with latte foam, covets leisure's aim
to truant the twitters of beat. Eddy lies: he's chaperoned
by yelps strafing indulgence. One more autocrat demurs:
one more autocrat is led to necrosis and rhymes of a *pars
pro toto.* Please listen to Eddy cranked by idlers, pestled
into mock bankruptcy, tranquilized by trivia and uplifts.

Legacy 0.0086%

The warp and woof of the last ghul, Eddy *Ra's al Ghul,*
the microbiome ghul as pure foie gras goose. Eliminate
his best way to achieve, aided by a Lazarus pit of dying
lifespans granted to quest the ghoul's head. Sora winced.
Sora's a corpse—eases her mother suffering with a germ
theory of contaminated keys. Retrieving Azazel, fortified
from hints of a prayer shawl, cops the now late marriage
of began, freed from the comic combat of his decfession
to be taught and listen. Why Azazel, late in Eddy rapture?
To legacy the outbreak of until. When will the shadows
leave these clichés? When he's injured and healed: high,
or poked with cute hat like *Death and the Maiden.* Why?
His sons are globes, uncracked future men of unfinished
Eddy. They won't fear blister pellets of a damaged lung.

Vendredi 13

Paraphilia write-in for the paraphilic days of Christopher
Clavius, adjusting the epacts of the moon when a 0.002%
of 365 days, 5 hours, 49 minutes and 12 seconds, redeals
the length between Eddy then or now. *Triskaidekaphobia,*
as blood chamber of 13 for the pomegranate and crucified.
Eddy's bad luck when he comes in three gifts of an Eddy
as the *triti* of a third king. They debate these taxonomies.
They hunt the classified disease of one valentine, despite
being naked in showers. They prod variants. They, they.
They roleplay in the matrix of partials and hybrid urges.
In some cases, he seeks the exhaust pipes of cars: fights
them as a He in a night of underwear. Everyone sneezes.
Everyone submits to dominical letters. Eddy's therapy
includes anti-androgen hormones, his growth-gain less.

Lumbersexual 3603216

In torts of distort, *The Book of Skin* punks Beatriz Viterbo
Daemon. She solves the woods, gatekeeps its buffed genes
of avenge—fines herself down to divert astrocartography
and mediocrity. She'll even dance with two naked chimps
in a cellar containing *The Aleph*. She loves Eddy's gestalt
lumbersexuality. He's a *Lord of Creation,* decked in brawn,
re.Bl.acl flannel and dyed red woodsy beard. May Beatriz
take a message? Eddy's out chopping down trees: Redwood
trees with one swing of his axe. His purple forehead tattoo
says "Sequoia Bust." Eddy then have an Amurkin whiskey
smile. Denim be the Patagucci puff jacket shroud, lumber
yard beard oil and suspenders. Day-code chacos, h.words,
scars and chain saws—E.d L/um boots a leathered skinny,
cocked with twigs and duct tape, to lotion his silky hands.

Harrow 2/3

To שְׁאוֹל with discrete structure halos and Ugaritic funerary
texts. Eddy belongs to a race of giant *Rephaim* instructed
to exterminate disfigured natives. Frack the cubits—suck
out dikes, the wellbores and chalk aquifers who use shade
to kill the ancestry of the *Malakuma.* This heap of stones:
this *tumulus,* this disc-shaped, ghost-cadre mong dolmen,
cede to cide. Seismic activity? An electromagnetic pulse?
No one but Eddy speculates as to the nature of this *limbus
patrum,* here in the middle two-thirds of harrowing's .666.
Over *inferos* and to grandmother's house he goes, freeing
captives of low confession. Nergal's *dunghill cock* gropes
Eddy's shade—input of algorithms as these new clichés.
A mockery of finite sets, cracking a unified frame, speaks
an unpronounceable Eddy name used to form agent nouns.

Surrogate 3006

Reify the deicide of nostalgia—in it these *thingifications*
come naturally, turning subjects into necks. Eddy's value
must include veins and the fetish of quiet. His thing-world
of bad behavior uplies anywhere else but here. Then, only
to neutralize atomism, cleaving to maps past the territory
of more lionhearted loss. Dis pathetic fallacies, unhinged
by the fake rapture of grief. Sentence him to a false logic
of *crawling foam*. Foam doesn't crawl. Eddy needs a real
pardon from a cloth-of-gold crocus. What da faque abhors
a vacuum on the passenger side of a fourteen line beauty.
Eddy cocks a *thirty-ought six*. Yes to his mowed trinities.
Yes to a *Tawḥīd,* when trios are lower than whole hands
of circumstance and turning points. Heart him *in medias
res*, in flash of *initio's* back, as Eddy is now lately pure.

Feline 9

Invading the chaste-souled in the *parahippocampal gyrus:*
Eddy codes memory. He's damaged. He want loved. Told.
They're lying because lying conjures a neuroscientist. Fear.
Hey, influencer, hear us/me: intends to mean, truly, he/Eddy
means not contrarily. Pretend not to be insulted, neutral see,
thereafter one pineal eye after all comments—years, to after
when it was considered no longer sad. Eddy never traveled
to avoid a prophet-pledge. Eddy's live in Luzern—prosodic,
no live in Babylon as logogram and never in doubt: go to it,
fill it now with the frequency of voice. These older attested
names snark the mark and bracket the square. *Sardis* laugh
loudly at a French *sardonique,* nullified to murder as a she
reason to love Eddy's glory hole. Only feet solve his to end
in nails, femfy or not or as cat-like laughter he for grinning.

Designate L115A3

Put the sniper in place, camouflaged in a fieldcraft
with an AWM 338, designated L115A3. Snipe birds,
wading birds, more so a pin-tailed snipe, the small,
stocky wader with its fizzing of a loud *tcheka* song.
Nineteenth century war-stile pieces follow quotes:
his enemy is demoralized in order to avoid his eye
fatigue and squad-level noises. When the doctrine
is deployed, calibers are used. Eddy spots a wage.
His close-contact team pummels a hutted village.
Posttraumatic stress disorder swoons in these guts
of smoothbore. Not as the real shakes, but as hype
pumped numb reaction to tisk. Squeeze the trigger
straight back—just the ball of the finger's prone
to a cheek, wrapped around Eddy's wankest arm.

Coulomb 1.602×10^{-19}

Storge and vice versa, to have variants and symbioses,
self-emptying, being together against menaces, doubly
impedes contrasted antonyms, coming with form: like
or just as good as the fraternal love of two Prehispanic
sculptures at the *Museum of Anthropology* in *Xalapa*.
Eddy boasts *Huastec* ancestry. He manders. Declothed
as if to court a late bond of clothing and blood trinities
were to override splits of uncandition. Not *paraphilia*.
Please no *erotomanias*. Eddy isn't patient as his ploy.
He lusts for neurons to keep his neck from bleeding.
Not an authentic *coq au vin* braised with a cube lard.
Eddy intimates intimacy's few unusuals. A negative
charge attracts some rare analogs: unlike him, feels
a hunger to continue its arousal of shutdown rage.

Manji 90

Swastikas and the Illuminati of unasked historicities:
here, equal in salvation for the Rabbis of Didáskalos.
Copper Scrolls in eleven caves of Khirbet Qumran,
speak of bones that do not die. Were his scribe only
Matthew, when he pointed at a House of Beelzebub,
reviled by the sign. Eddy hearts a role in the Petrine
doctrine. He laps *sangreal* for has one role: *ex bello
pax,* but loves the antiquity of *batayles.* Eddy wars
an open fist, battles open firsts on thumbless palms.
No one's neighbor. No one's complaint, quantized
later than most dissidence. By fiat of consent, Eddy
wills not to be forgotten. Genomes are genocide's
luck. Is Eddy lucky? Only if infinitely curved away
from insufficient funds. He pleads to make a deposit.

Foudre 12305

The bond duties of matrimony, defacto, mull or coil; spouse cohabit the sanction required of other, divided if affected to a base fault of divide. Eddy's liable party breach. Eddy's lift of the weight of burden. Ur-nuptial judges ratify squawks to avoid collision. Transponder code or wedding day? Eddy knocks for a decade, a gif of seconds explained in stills. Nothing settles but a raw loss of gain. How about the custody of emergence? No, not among tiny no-faults who grant just a mere hearting pass. Key factors buckle. The in-laws of gonads break. Break her, way center right to concession—the barest of suffice breaks the silence of proof. Eddy lifts from the married three to own Eddy. Uncontested U of one, finally neither sequential nor proved betread fodder.

Job 1:6

Let him be wed with the dew of heaven, an iron band
or brass knuckle to a platinum ring's left ring finger:
braided ring of reeds or gimmel ring worn for double
ceremonies—consecrated Eddy by decree of watchers:
Daniel's watchers who misunderstood the Masoretic
text. The *egrégoroi* fall from the fifth heaven where
the fall is later unfallen and coupled with these *Sons
of God.* The *nephilim* may still count in a few years,
but it's unlikely. Eddy's gone drastic. Who's Eddy's
titulary person? Only his sacred bride—his consort
of Inanna's fourth proximal digit, his weaker *digitus
quartus,* heart-shaped when two left hands of she/he
form the outline of a heart, less clasped by the thumb
than a rigged jubilee, dismantling all divine threats.

Apology 399

Eddy corrupted his female wards and poured molten lead down their throats, searing their bowels, forcing them to strip naked and put on stink-clothes of *tunica molesta*. He revered a she of spiked chins. Eddy got off on liquid fire, his beauty as a she cased in orange fire. There are penalties for distant intercourse. Later, years beyond rigor mortis, Eddy is burnt alive as luz bone. Nothing is burnt—the bone-bit of spine's body is all Eddy needs to breathe without lungs. His breath is a Southern California crow's caw as heated March of early haze. Palm and pine bicker to become lucky heirs to an epiphany of rain. Both admit to being dry. There's a year left to Eddy's truancy. Will care gloss his medium? Will his mock-killers oblate his naiveté?

Coefficient .916

A lady tour bus of 80+ ladies parks at the Harborside
Restaurant—Eddy's mother pours over agitated suns,
redeems a jipped past of failed husbands. Eddy looks
like the sepulcher of a wizened cartouche: looks like,
but is an image left behind, a *jipocolypse*, rolled into
one huge jip, when universes jip coefficients to .916
of a prefect one. Eddy's double dies in the childhood
of age, dies in normative reasons of clause. A jipper,
but nota womb of the earliest ancestry. Eddy's triplet
may not live past his muscle's atrophy. Coefficients
summon the world's end: just summon, not then real,
by the same amount, will cause the axis of perfection
to become a memory gland of fraction. To continue,
because we must in complexity's gut-lacking closure.

Geisha 794

Eddy won't live past a dythic *ygnyfycance*, hys brain's
cycle of romance won't live que when she dies. Eddy's
life won't skee past his delabeled quf. He dehumanizes
won't? Here, in/or/mong dyssocyative's ess-than-human
simulations to increase a last-ditch effort to appeal a one
death sentence of oppeal. Love's ubiquity overreaches as
an offed mother of sundials. Eddy contributes to recipes
of a hollandaise parasol with white-powder facey rouge
lips. Relimit upheaval's meme. Eddy is sexlees. His wyfe
lives arsed in her parents all day beyond seam, be.yon/d
sum: s-a-m-e, what's? Eddy's a cardinal water trine/trin,
a tad past fifty-two, lucky to be lyvely in a geiko fantasy,
o-shaku, kabuku, accentuating the nape of the neck, still
styred by rapture's canon of momoware and split potch.

Déjà Vu 1307

Opposed to a round one of wooden structures used
for beheadings that slid up and down in red grooves
of the uprights, Eddy now prays to a *Halifax Gibbet*
to silence his petty crime. Where's the body named
Murcod Ballagh, severed from his torso near 1307?
The condemned is lying on a bench. Axes are sharp
and notably gruesome. The axe of a covenant axes
puckered faith between antithetical genders. Eddy
improves the accuracy of holy incest. A divinity's
the guilty party, your honor, not these confiscated
archetypes, lured by registration. Sensing a burial,
Eddy avoids inflicted pain. It's an on/off button at
the back of the rig. As quaint as the colloquial buzz
of an I/it tag, his future atrophies seeing refor now.

Dorian 1891

Eddy's *apologia* is that he never dies, at least never
as a goth. Eddy's beauty is pure *hēdonē,* pure nubile
libertine, liquid as textured oil paint. Eddy postures
in vain to trick like Sybil Vane. No trick, but dingy
spots in low-rated feeds of a now in stills and subtle
sneers of all but cruelty: Omni, as true Latin prefix
but minus one, the mother of all hatreds, cruelty. It
will tear as Eddy Omni, but in tears dull as prussic
acid, so hurt by the love of swallowing *À Rebours.*
He searches for a table setting and then to dispose
of the body with nitric acid. Is peril that outdated?
Is it so purely without motive as to trend a minute
and recede into these undying feeds? Defluencers
act in parts written for somebody else's changers.

Tumescent 25,000

Sexus, or ὁμός as a hormonal stiff of suspension,
tightens in the waistband, in these early uterines,
factored to stretch the pant. Nothing plays erode
the variable as much as Eddy's penile census. He
substitutes Károly Mária Kertbeny's *homophilia*
for a queer primordia of weighted ergo slurs, gay
in vogue but deprived of our wristed *soumission*.
Can Eddy proscribe beyond the penalty of death?
Lieblingminne untranslates the erected man-man
love as Hadrian, Antinous and/or Eddy's frottage
of sacred outercourse: mostly among versatile's
frot-elected. Dr. Frenulum concedes to a tissue
of stimulation. How about a ridged band's delta
teabagging the emptied era, passing in and out?

Ludus 1957

Tender, tricked harmonic of root plus bass intervals
of a feathered soft, harmonizes a minute beforehand.
The joint of concord. The *harmonia* of pitch, clearer
than any *traité de l'harmonie* aired by a night's notes
of misreading. Lost hagiographies of St. Contrapuntal,
conjure the critics of music. Eddy hated criticism. Not
hate, not the ripped modal commands of notate, Eddy
remained unchanged by ratios. Surprised by a rough
factor of obvious song? No Madame Grave, Eddy's
having a busy afterlife in parallel intervals of thirds
and sixths. An aging mortician forbids the early use
of the tritone. Eddy chimes in as new musicologist
of a *musica ficta* without notes. Not notes, two cut
nostrils as face-holes hearing sound as dead smell.

Retrieve 2006

Eddy won't condemn the *universalis negativa* to become
a mock replica of himself. He won't let *oratio enunciativa*
be both prequel and sequel. He can't be as true at the same
time as a *subcontrariae* is true to contradiction. Medieval
logicians utter *subalternation* and *superalternation*. Eddy's
hair is in question: clippers or scissors? If this is a man, he's
done nothing: *se questo è un uomo*. Interest in him is now
increased to a pulse of a clichéd pun. Some man is just, one
quality is the *subaltern* of a universal statement of in same
quality: some A is B and no A is B implies some A is not B
in Eddy's logic of wrong. The fiered are the chasen people.
They won't collect unemployment benefits, annexed from
the wages of loss in these weak contradictories, rendered
as pure loss pointing towards the *dialectica* of not exist?

Vacate 60

How less dead is the grammar of recall? Surprised
at the degree of deterioration, Eddy eats renaissance.
Liberal amounts of cheese and dressing prior later
than public option. D. Eddy is the one who knocks.
The death instinct of survival overeats these sugar
relatives. D. Eddy never had milkshakes and cokes.
The landlard must give the tonant at least three days
to carrect the priblem. If the tonant has lived in the
pramises for more than one year, the landlard must
provide at least 60 days' netice to vacate. Buffoons
empty the vassel. They are the chasen. The breach
of anywhore but here conjures ghosts in machines.
When will the gads of caseloads concede? Groins
of a tear syncopate. Eddy dies before omniscience.

Friday 1306

Eddy holds his body in fetters like a prisoner. What
dissolves this compact? A trek round the wide circle
is in need of grace far from the grace of ascetic piety.
Carry it back from North-Eastern Hellas to Magna
Graecia. Eddy's due for adoption and bliss released
from the Republic of Constraint. Engineers lure late
suns from the crow-shrieked afternoon. Suns? More
than one sun, Ephebe? Yes, inconceivable sun ideas
of both Phoebus and Ephebe. How sick is a cranked
tag never named for a flourisher? As sick as the red
malignancy of a first idea recalled by one ordinary
man. He sees *myositis* on the drought water of his
dirty mirror. Eddy's gorgeous in his gut as faddier
to Descartes. Diarrhea claims second Friday earths.

Ιησοῦς 333

Who is already deeply in debt to the Templars? How
about Eddy as *Hospitaller Grand Master* Foulques
de Villaret. How simple is expiration? Kill Sir Eddy
before we admit to *paraskevidekatriaphobia.* Eddy
won't admit to being a Moor and loving *Al-Andalus.*
Nothing placates like olives and salted fishic skins.
Duck, it's the Nazarene in Mary's Well. Eddy lives
for the irregular in Greek and the additional vowel.
Henry Church is so shy. A godliness preceded us,
tells the vacant story of why our story matters. Me
matters. Me tragedy. Me bare board offed by Eddy.
More ones will truly love him: *coulisse bright-dark*
red or mansard when dumb violence, now subside
fullback, supine, three-meter lateral bursts more.

Chorister 1931

Paternal, sartorial antefixes with sarcophagus lids,
is Eddy now secreted intact beneath his beads, bots
and flasks? Cumfic *denu 'mā* dovetails in as jumble,
recurving the slide. Petrichor flows in older Eddy's
pre-arthritic veins. He's an aerosol can scented with
a hint of rigor mortis, sprayed in the palms of an exit
strategy. Exit through the *oubliette* with the higher
ceiling. The hatch cedes the epilogue to a covenant
of body holes rendered hollow in Old High German.
Increase the flank of the chorister who adds a hole
to the holes of a holed Eddy. He's the *one of fictive
music* rising from the organed maestro. A chorister?
Yes, the scam of *diviner love* snipped from the flow
of low expectations, begs the defeat of Mr. Daemon.

Oxford 17

If wiki *tortrix* in genus of a moth, occurs *gravis*,
then into that true muscle condition of the weak
goes we: Eddy forces W.S. to exert a less jected
versal of Chanzy's or Jyms' *vi-lexia* to ἀσθένεια,
wife-rite as arted remorse of a two *dfrau*-lung's
choke. The Return of Hegemons bares primary
lags and nerve-sags, not occluded by E's *cento*
corseted I-Lizabeth. Edward Da Emon/Edward
De Vere—Eddy Daemon/Eddy Devere, elbow's
slip-re to stingy for fifteen more days of an *arte
athletica*. Eddy jousts blunted tips. What/a/luck
imips the contractile forces of the Will of Simul.
Admit it, it's true as last resistance of play: ask
an end/up/giving to these Trusties of Extremes.

Nym 7

How much older is the 7th oldest Earldom of Don
than Eddy's Don de Arris? Seeded jousters snoop
the accelerated race of dead fathers. Where's a raped
annuity to relieve got/heirs/to/carry/his/name? E.D.,
when the seat impudes the surrogate faith reformers,
beats cosmography into the science of the brain—so
new as to pop the pure late glam of the hand. That's
not new texts the Inviolated Wife, not adjunct says
Daut Havisham of R. Splaton. Breach *liti* is subject
to the mage. This suit against files of one yucks off:
friends just next-doored, are far less crafted not tobe
a seismograph for lip-words caught queering a Son
of Jejune. Jejune's the *melek* of the messiah's heart
sold in foreclosure. It's a lovey *nym*, isn't it Eddy?

Thule 1918

Ultima Thules of last straws are a mandrake root
with ovate leaves arranged as rosary, bell-shaped
and milfed for runic priests, led by Padre Eugene
Ics, second cousin to Harvey the Rabbit. Yellow
and orange berries from the axils of Mandragora
plants from Israel, are heated by Metal Halides.
Racial hygiene has always been the quest, here,
in Hyperborea, in the District of Columbia, near
the reached vista of Nurica, sung in Old Norse.
Then Eddy appears in the Atlantis of shoal mud
and claims himself the Logographer of the Spear,
omni-mentee, inheritor of the sunflower poked
into the *Body of Christ*. Eddy demurs: Christos
is Harvey, the gentle phantom of extermination.

Lion 46

God was invented by Ludovico Mazzolino to image
the obese satisfaction of *caritas* and terror. Is posture
the mother of the first rule? Only if the ontic abstracts
are nouns. A chaffed sky of fêted clouds crows argot:
a secret language of in-outed laws, first *les argotiers,*
then as group of hackers, a little less than the loveless
half-hull of a 46-gun ship of the line *tigre.* The Lion
of Judah is the carotid artery of an alter cockered I-I:
mock-solemn, the father of firsts with fingered palms
and bubbled thumbs. Eddy is the pure gum of lovely:
he's the Saxon Fort of Zion in a mock-Galilee's 2nd
coming of wait/to/see the athlete he bears crowding
the patron of the pure. Remember the prolonged light
of weakened gleaners? These doors and balustrades?

Human 72

Human, the metabolic waste, the four chambers,
the *cor/kardia* so simple in frizz and *logoclasody*
as to buy tickets to the Epigones of Roundelay.
None of these fourteen are English. No revivals
invite *emoji's* to exit a finally true *polyarmony*.
Not one asks the lux/in/oxygen to grow sons.
He passes the left ventricle and is pumped out
through the aorta's harmolodic *deworded erbu*
and repossessed—stop the car at 72 beats per
minute. The Aegis of Mandate is ineligible to
the well-born, to the race, stock and kin: alone,
wiped by the sham of the moist eventide, Eddy
is left to a midsternum's camps of resistances,
deflected and pitted as a half-prophetic Uman.

Babalú 401

Why is the true Eddy witness named Tadeusz Babalú?
Why is the name *Babalú-Ayé* translated as Father, Lord
of Eddy? Toss a curative ailment, link-loving the feared
demic of cowry shells. He never claimed victims, never
demanded that they be infected by the outcasted shines
of since. Do you remember Lucille Ball's Ricky? Club
Tropicana? The seventeen candles? Tadeusz is a hop's
jump to safety: all hail the Eddy of Desi Arnaz, synced
with tens of thousands of devotees honored in *grimage*.
Stop a dying of exposure on a beach where he is badly
scarred by crabs. Summon the nurses of back/to/health.
He's protected from disease. His lair dresses an *Orisha*.
Secrecy and revelation won't do. The pedagogical guide
is read, he means the lauded mentor of these new lungs.

Cluster 34

Clustered, easy-lit to caress a light-*Iocese* divided
into four—Eddy's bulk is blooded to receive *venae
cava* goodbying the dumpster's throne. Carbon me
if sustained *releunt* an aorta me: dies the heartbeat
of stasis with the slow transport of a thoracic meme
all body parted to *pumpsto* a scheme. Can you hear
the breath of the nasal cyclops? Eddy will jam into
a late *stele* at a rest stop to wave adieu to a silvered
bonz. 2015 is 1615 *ʃeɪkspɪər*. Stratford-pon-Avony's
Sierra Vista decedes a fuhgeddaboudit towards air.
Eddy the Apex drives in air of flight *cum* tarpaulin.
Eddy's maudit will source the on/on viscera of go,
colored with so/last/centuried *coeur* of a one man.
Mrs. Vereiosky heard it early—34 years ago, ibid.

Circle 1987

Eddy began as a mistoke, a dispossession no link
nor hyperlink could absolve with lesser degrees
of work. He refused to work his born a *Subtitulos
Español* too handsome for women and for men.
From Vilna this Jascha Heifetz of the Daemon
is neither from Andalusia nor Vilna—absolute
pitch sprinkles the rounded lie of orange hymns
in e-flat major: grave, *adagio cantabile*, English
and Scotch-Irish with a smidgen of 19th century
ashkenazic pitch. Say Vermin King of genteel
classes? Vermin begs the unbacome—so out,
so not *au courant*. Just one more day without
the politics of identity, for politeness sake? No,
make the fetish count, simple, mash/d cuckold.

Emoji 12×12

Eddy's in a 12×12 pixel grid, the sequenced two
byte of encoded threes: not the set aside blocks
of a legacy set, but freed from a caged showrat's
truancy—only to feature a draft of clean U+1F3x
dingbat *partur* in burrowed *urthers*. Eddy catches
the bacteria shed in liquid droplets during a Paris
operation in 1897. Paris, or tissued out in Chicago,
mits bright with abaneion? How airborn are blue
masks? Such *nitation*, such false magick: mercy
me Ercy or non-woven and discarded after easily
transferred to droplets of Eddy's misspelled name.
He landed in bacteria, sneeze-wearing gilded Lily
to please the anyones of her. He can't stay to milk
the light, udders squeezed for *Eretz*. Come back
Rebbe Daemon your *tigrons* are buxic in where.

Cast 2237

Casting the common rupestric then, plucks the native
nous of recalling Ya and Worky jigging with shades
of the pale mausoleum—call the flutterby the head's
hinged felt this once before. Try and see the portals
through the grime of serial joy: the heart's sweet bad
cess' *tu me taquines* faked to be true. I hear the *ekes*
of take it longer than any daughter of breed should
take the *liefest* pose. I hear congas beat the Cossacks
of dabble and repent. Eddy's now a *selfloud* of the I:
I-grow, hearted larger than Ukrainian *pysanka* dyed
the single color of anointed color. Mary Magdalene's
basket serves as a repast. Friend Simon the Peddler
on Morse in *Chivary*. They are divinity's rare shells,
each committed to Eddy living for a few matte yelps.

Gonad 2001

Haine-hass fested to *j'ai la haine:* not me, not a motor
cortex in the frontal lobe of imperious rage and frontal
gyrus. They. They're The Imperious Bunnies of Inertia
from which Eddy ben Mediator heals to kill an undead
Hebrew to return to his sons. Rip apart these unbiased
willings that know that no *urderer ath ternal:* counting
falling bodies to one hundred and fifty four may die out
in mosquito amber. Less than three will have pituitary
glands removed from what is not free and limitless: he
grew tissue and actin that rew past a chonged posture.
Respite in safe havens fail. It's cardiac and smooth. A
witch hunts emasculation. Nothing appeases lifetimex
of hate, however justified and gutted of scale purpace.
Blame lack of *apologia:* blame what reomptied in 2001.

Esperanto 1895

The *be-éhtml* codes of dark language keyboards
help misconstrue the empirics of L.L. Zamenhof's
Esperanto as *Internacia Lingvo* of moded weight.
Eddy lurks in an antechamber guarded by goyles
named Ludwik and Lejzer. He works at Theater
Białystok on Sunday nights, gleaning an extract
from his 1895 letter to Nikolai Borovko. Biolitak
outposts of antiquity spark his halos: not clinical,
not outsized, not even as a motive's unseen goal.
Still courting these imps of obfuscation? Dodgy
ball-cuts aren't they? Eddy needed. Is kneaded
to form gauges in ends. The warded *appi* leans
into me. Neither of us are prostrate to the hedge
as bets that Eddy's price drop is circumstantial.

Eve 99,000

Mitochondrial Eve back from all bombs converge
to reenact our global kill quads? Sulfur, mustardy
greed cells unlike dead namesakes from green 99%
to yellow 99,000% blistered lung-snub of warfare:
sulfur mustard synthesized by treating dichloride
with ethylene. Homo *heidelbergensis* is our scam,
our Syria older than the rusted screws of ulcerative
colitis in sidmoid colons dating Eve to necrophagic
leaving groups formed by the *agnatic* mother-line,
in repossessions of versatile hands. Poverty's uni
prime is dyslexic. It refuses the binary lag. Hunger
is the peptide of pang, the blood-sugar of an extra
severe skinned scarcity of the great mother of lack,
with her hirsute gnat-squad crawl up her pink arm.

Grimm 209

The white hum of ceremonial magick, dusted grim
in the grime of stasis courts the Æon of Horus/ace,
charmed by the ancestry of black curtains, reveres
the oversoul of dust. Does anyone hear the hollow
of a classic? *Arbeit macht frei's* metalwork signals
an innocent Lorenz Diefenbach? From virtue, fraud
and a friendship with Mr. Jacob Grimm. Eddy loves
Rose Edith Kelly. He finishes her sentences. Rosey
agency's the final work, no more final than a fraud
of *Aiwass*. Eddy still cares deeply. He splits bodies.
He collapses the *Ordo Templi Orientis*. Themela's
a true bitch devoted to the Thelamites of One: hurt
ones who live on hurt, emptied of source for aging
pissed. Decay ins rot and sources betrayal. Sorgive.

Rarity 88

A gene called *Transgene* is injected in his offspring because his genetic codes are similar to genetically modified mice. Don't mince the alphabets of skin with the rarefied squealings of an inversed passion. The statutes of rare father a lethal raider of a now, or soon to be inarticulate selfhood, collects public opinion like a simple need to collect. Into an early stage mouse embryo refuses to leave. Mayed heat is humid, is the novel to exeunt our rat. 88 rarities give the *errata* slip the slip. Sunrise is at 5:20 AM. The HIV Index is as low as two transgenic Eddys never seen in this approach. Hardly rare: *ardly re* nor *aar ar* to the dusted amputee. Scarcity's lack. Fetch antibacterial soap. Alternative is scrubbed.

Morse 1923

His *unsub* name is Acute Coryza or Peter Precog.
Pick the pepper, the pickled pepper of hey diddle
diddle I feel you looking away from your research.
No one dies the voice of the age: no one nor when
scrappers roamed to pick up our rusted hvac trail.
The imitators invent. My *longueur* to invent, say
in a while, dons a *spodik*. Eddy can't stop staring
at the shrug. His work is neither closed by snips
nor casket lengths. Why did vexes come so easy?
The *pharmatog* cure is gritty with the grey scraps
of metal. Is Eddy's blue guitar tuned 1923 yellow?
Is it tuned to West Rogers Park? He imps Y-ris
as the shtetl light in three golems of wiring skin
comfort hung habilements of zero sensations.

Listener 150%

The opposite of dystopia is *pherō*. Really? On what
planet, Lieutenant Eddy "Illian" Ell, do gifted kids
jones for *Cortexiphan?* Rap da steal Ms. Beta Moxy.
Lega of the Ol, Eddy croons, is emptying rust-glass
in the alley. No one dare mock the Ol. No one dare
cross the beauty of gates. Eddy's a reverse-empath,
hearted, kind ones, to pressure the belly of two feel
be sure. I'm in love with Hannah Barthedoor: ways
were extreme. When was Eddy a man? When it fell
apart I knew that I would live to don a tallit, or use
it as a laptop cover. Hobble a daven? Later at night,
no. The Mercenaries of Bolic impede three tenders.
A lepsis? A clarity of tone in the PSE? It may stand
for nothing. We can't help it—the brux-lifting rays.

Capet 16

Gamesh, you here? To rip out the morphed ectos,
or say belt down some new *treyf*? Hardy har/her,
Har-Edi the Platypus. No one's jacking implants.
It all went cafluey when you backed brain wave
receivers in ears. Did you patent extropy? Come
now bud, can't give an inch on memeplexes? No,
+um. You're it. You're the true stink of genity. I,
credo. I, countdown to the final boredom. Give it
up for Manuel "Manny" Hands, the one working
the gears from the asylum. He wears a Louis XVI
culottes with straps and buckles. He and Gamesh
stop to buy t-shirts with a zebrafish and a tadpole.
Somebody stole the *Raiment of Pleasure*. Eddy,
was it you? It's a mild case of acid repluxi, chill.

L.H.O.O.Q. 1919

Enhancers in the false root of *trep,* shift stigma
to a new rebel army to combat the Bytleucids they
had become: bicep-ripped stewards led by donors
of anti. ACCAB in the lurch—to install—to patch
the hawkish drive with its umbrella of focus. What
role does Eddy play on campus? He's a late most
notable no-show, unbound to fail his outruly stint
in nootropics. Here's a therapeutic window. Look,
no L.H.O.O.Q. at his readymade ease of felt, *objet
trouvé* and lipgloss heart. I see his thin handlebar
moustache, his hair gel and curling iron. His task
saliency has improved. He won't be radicalized
with selective memory. He won't be a *toparch,*
resolute in his role as a last among the parities.

Chiroptera 777

Vocal folds: tongue, palate, cheek, lips and muscle, striated smooth and mesodermal. Frank Yicksee is here to cop the yal for stored foraging of a later cut trance. The era of extermination was just mourned on West Morse for the *desmodus rotundus*. Themly were pros and cons, but they could disappear with the caped junk: too much line, too much of a line's *buis*. Xalapas don't. Stints in possession don't care again. Quiver simplicity is the key, gut-huddled fix to hear a *gymnopédie* through rotted paint chips. A cry's subdomain's spread ear digits of a sonic blit: it's a bat name Alastair. Not Aleist. Alast Jack with arms of stare at him. How gentle is *acked* nurture? Enough to rate a fresh fish grotto? F.R. Yick cares.

Lazarus 16:19-31

PHWY brought back to life, rising from Ed Ones,
you see, resembling what was most left out: super,
supersized holy thorns of undiagnosed privilege. I
eat horseradish with kosher vinegar and salt. Okay,
Eddy will not wave adieu. He's all about pealing.
He's not managing symptoms. Grope expletives.
Be the wizard. Be a new catalogue of a domestic
unisist. Say come back, but largely through such
matters which don't concern Eddy's quick-to-hit
penchant to expose. We noticed, as if a "we" bred
a softer fael. Was the choice well-hailed? Yes/no
pilgrim, it was Š'ôl the dull/spirited stand/in for
the EDDY writing hybrids. Cock an experience
in real time. I know Eddy's intent—bust inside.

Sequester 11%

Please sequester our repose. You posing? Who hells
the bastard line? Pretty.feee/lyng.poe/try.a.dra./ma
with the life Eddy lived: your 360 degrees no don'ts
the sincerity. Eddy, that he will slide in and out or in
ears to be heard with earplugs, sexes recall, but don't
listen to me. Water vapor is a gaseous state. It drips.
Right the wrong of *humidex*. Given the volume's air,
Eddy picks 30 grams per cubic meter. Mass mix our
ratios. Out of it, how the machine of normalcy skins.
Refend norma.lcy, the gland as extreme. I am gland.
I am when *pulliaen* Eddies balk, forgive, bend: sorry,
we embers get an *ould* moist as grime. Assword *gpk*:
simp? How cute can this be? You have no idea. NO.
RIP: roughly 11%. M Gam is tidy. Dress Ed: proof.

Alphanumeric XYZV>5

Input is x. Output is y. The set is z. The manifold is v.
We have reached the regressand and minimize game
for alphanumeric logins, oiled in these focus-killing
television shows. Five-eye drills blind to a vacant
blur, gorging on binaries and pissed at the solution.
How long past rock blood was he supposed to live?
Long enough to curl density and be buried in grime.
The mulberry's lobed shoots turn dark purple: ripen,
drop and mix with Chicago dirt. Rat holes multiply.
Entropy is a rotted log, mounted like a pagan god
against a pink and grey chipped garage. The ashes
of dead parents are white-fruited cultivars. Eddy's
on the brink of fertility and new abs. Mind control
is dead. He exercises the lot and makes ixi claims.

Mathewson II

Micro aggressions rise blank to ascension: ur-cut,
savage, to omit the dupe—(re)emerges to femme
a skin of guts an oblique attraction. Earl Shoepeg
sucks Eddy's soul. Earl's an Eddy rumpologist ('st):
burned as impurity, agent of rapture in alchemy's
concrete trellis: McEddy coins Earl. The televised
repulsed (s)form improvises vises of imp. Scranton
is the iron-scrappy of a wicked non-future: ture, re,
rrrgrrl—pure skin of a song of girl hears only me.
My/our head: sheer paralysis: imps of consensus.
Eddy is far afield. The serious of piss and norms.
Beauty of bone. No wonder/wander. He passes
gaunt, love a miner from to mine her/him after
to love cum Earl's logic washes a duck's glee.

Danger 1026

Eddy courts danger: evangelical rabbi, traced in impurity
and flavor—cereal grains of taters and lips or mid-sugars
and fruits. Eddy jones for a revenge move, not mix-mixed
or served chilled. Eddy's poems are grafts of intent: instant
allegation, distilled and postfix of a shejen called *gorzałka*
(from the *Old Polishgorzeć* as to burn), merchant cleanse
to storm the grain, dilutes water—glossed as to "rectify
corn-spirits" of the test. Stop staring at me romance/me.
How many meals in Poland are served? How are lights?
The *acqua vitae* of hear: *bimber, brennvin,* Eddy drinks
the new beat of increased purity. Beat down. Beat hip: ip,
it, me—me real, me high, it, when cease ceases to be it,
Eddy's an *horilka,* lust awakened from rye breaking she
as steady he gropes a rural stint with orange pulverizer.

Mandy 1972

The Amanda of *gerundive*, non-finite as *portandus*,
is carried to futurity with the help of Lord Ray. Boxes
are the stables of transport, or simply, worthy to love
the golden mean of moderation. In light conversation,
the canon of closure cuts a thin Mandy with a Mickey
Finn. Before fat and happy, I hated the grope. *Chloral
Hydrate* was a designer jean. They *doctorated* curves
in the renaissance of mental health. Eddy knew Manda
as a keeper of the priory, before nothing felt measure.
Now, Amanda ranks in the name: Milly-Molly-Mandy.
Mandy's *shema* heard handy in oz of night, late dark
because the emerald is drank to expose a mere behind
the curtain of return. Farce plays manner. Farce kicks
a goat-girl escaping the flock. Among an only left to.

Beacon 417

Eddy rigs his hair and texts *trichophilia* to his use/me Am
Parsand. Eddy grooms like a bonobo. I want you to suck
the thermal insulation of my scalp-vide cooling your soak
hair—cue to repro, to adornment's runaway—this Eddy
andro of lust and trait. Select Eddy, he became a sexed
nazarite: Samson by example or Gaelic Irish in a lobby.
Pick Eddy stiff in avenge for the ponytail, plait, or bun
bonbon of the *Merovingians*. The scalp is the lower ugh
of bulk and hip, chin level skirt swaying in beach wind.
The longest hair terminates the butt. Don't trim slender
waist. Don't worry the disheveled slick black shirt. You
stopped talking to me. Eddy embarrassed you. Vine curls
are as sexy as Saul of Tarsus becoming Paul. His anagen.
His terminal hair, hormonic, friggin *tubare* with a comb.

La Plume 1868

Sum-zero gain equal to YHWH, INRI or INBI, be-to pumped by the *equilibria* of erro in requence or glove. Each kept node gropes its advent in La Plume, Transylvania. PX transliterater of iron sacrifice cuts Eddy as Chaimy ben Kristobal, augments a bucolic wedge sinker as "gentlemen hurler." The Holy Grail is culmed in anthracite and burnt for sesquicentennial: severe, stable and sprayed with blue dye. How deperfect these players, how fracked clean with pressurized liquid. This is more Eddy than wellbore, more wildcatter than nonfession of self. Author, author—did we admit that onity was ampty? How about three individuals playing a normal game? Is trinitarian unity ampty? Our enion is ampty. This is our valance payoff, our fadeaway. Living of a recessed sriumph, picks only one devout Eunuch. The reset is balk to toss out the control pow of tability gains.

Pollock 44

Eddy drips like a Non-Euclidian fly, swinging from a punctured bucket. A stick with a protocol? Steal brushes? Basting syringes to sauce a spicy marinade? "Tubes" Daemon drips house paint. Gestural lines eye travel, are less vicious. Paint runs, ambulates on the ground. Far less than dripslash mark, seduction's breasts lick the Navajo's sand—no one is held culpable. Not the native strains of orgasm nor the "sterile kitchen," underpaints a norm. Eddy's resin-based, synthetic, an alkyd full of fatty acids. Coat the form-fixed entry of slide, the maleic formula of n-butane. I concede the stage to Eddy, give him an Archie McPhee, Instant Audience. Options: applause, crickets, rimshot or boo. Is Eddy Jack the Dripper? He prefers trowels and knives. I don't prefer. I demur to polyol. Ebad. I demur to Eddy Daemon. What class of polyols are low sweeteners? We share each other in glycitol.

Pansexual 1917

Eddy's bi, attracted to derision, *mosexu* in Pitman Shorthand:
an abugida in the language of Swampy Cree. Vowels, abjads,
or the absent optional fulfills an equal. Pick an either/or type.
How pan is bi? Or equate, but not *exclu*. *Grees* of both. PanS
is as PanSex. Ceed poly, or *eed oly*, rejects a binary fem/hem.
We cater to this *ophos* as if our mastered *isexu* were *erosexu*.
Give it up for Eddy "Polquee" Daemon, punk *roflex* of dark
n-ders. His botch is an oxual—a certain Ames Obia Bianga,
cut part femme fatale, ladyboy and greased hunk. At *Nogra,*
in the Back Bay, they party with a penile plethysmograph.
They toke on the strain of gauge and down inflatable cuffs.
This film stimuli of phallometry and vagines of a silk labia,
consort the fall. Curve *pathols* little hotties. Eddy and Ames
are *etehom,* cuming *tasy* and bated by the lure of an *ariab*.

Limbic 53

Roperty, n-titled en masse, *avec* three, hits a *muneras* of climax. Our p-vic of zones are *nomic*: be up *luxuria* in Bost, Massachusetts. Oper Oseas is awake, ignites fire: knot, wheel in the Museo del Commo. *Cave Deus Videt*, void of counsel and *discipulo* with these recent dendrochronologies of darker rites. Muses are *mousai*. Eotia Edette wears an etiolated veil. Oper and Eotia are demons, not daemons, ogre-like, varied as Meta and Para: -philia, or agape and a *pithet* to cauterize the wound. Stop the trick roleplay, Madame Vestie, or (sic) *anoia*. Enteric neurons are gutless *mobilite?* Here's Sonora the Wizard. The fourth in the trinity. Oper and Eotia, are our Romeo and Juliette. Who? Sonic the hedgehog. Ormic the avocado. Eddy eel?

Kalashnikov 7.62×39

Narcocorrido, or hop of an accordion-based polka:
he gone. Dead, the demon hellraiser, late to graves,
fuams da *rame*. I broke through the Welco/Ur. Eddy
urt a mute rapport, thug *unt* a whatup esse *oly-dily*.
He fated, hypered in insult, in the fleas of *tianguis*
and the romp of *teño*. How lyrical is *polvo*? His ax
is the *cuerno*, the Kalashnikov with a tuning fork.
Add a green bird's eye, a yellow madame Jeanette
and some red cayenne peppers, and all word rivals
are sliced up as *al pastor*. Why *corridos enfermos*,
these mock sonnets of insanity? Is the alternative
worth fighting for? No Jesús Rẹy Daemon. *Nada
es más importante.* The poet is a hitman—mortar
and pestle, pumping cartridges in dummy bodies.

Melancholy 1514

Malaina C. Daemon is self-wiled, *wist, moro* or *ent*
in saturnine. Eddy's ears are Dürer's, classified four
among shot biles and *lugere*. The liquefied humours,
xenoglossy of a tongue *langue,* tissue grey primacies
of thrust. Ina's *merencolie* is Albrecht's furry collar.
How truncated is the rhombohedron? Not as devout.
Merry, much merrier than c/ulted, sports a Romany
scarf and Jacobean plume, cums on the frontispiece.
The human skull has an hourglass—purse and keys,
sipping on Tito's, seltzer and winged figures. Cut
the woodcut in the men's bathhouse nor block out,
block cutters cut block—a hot, chiseled *burin* stirs
the lithic flake of murder. Hit 'em when they move.
The apostle wears bodycolor. The new turf negates.

Necrotic 1952

Caustic simp, diced to stick, his body dys *ad hominin*,
as *extre* is to mist. The simp's *dermatillomania* picks
at the sores, comps the *ulsive* of cis comorbidity. Ex
is to *coriat* what dis is to order: words are abscesses,
typed by severe picking. Eddy will need a skin graft.
Eddy's the caustic simp, the one who picked his neck
raw to expose the carotid artery. Carbuncle, yo. Boils,
yo. Pustules, yo. Gang is to *grene* what fa is to *tality*.
Chill or fever E. Trachy Trach. Don't worry. It's just
cell death in fasciitis poetry. Hey *anachrons*, do you
hear subterranean? Yea/no. It was subcutaneous. Not
home. Not sick. Not blue. Archives infect The Ronics
of PreCanon. In pre lies post. No one wrote the code
this way before. No one drew bacteria from a SSID.

Vesper 1662

Expop me a *tital* courtier to the Corpus Zone of A.
These Mafiosos of Mediocrity don't die in bit rates
of an apostle—stello+από/apo hit send. Their *missio*
is a ground state of cesium, to ignite the air. A few
more to easy purity. A few more to the Ember City
of Pyrophoricity. The offended petition The Ears.
It's a matter of *aith minations*. How similar they
are to the Mafiosos with their romantic allusions
to analogs. Goodput is Godput. Eddy loves Ana
Phora. Ana carries the back forward, works intel
at the Corpus Zone of A. Eddy texts the offertory.
Ana communes her compline to the tone of weeks.
Vespers are *kippurs*—evensong is *Even Flow*. Yeah.
Linewidth of nonzero hear my way—I/me *Expop*.

X-Peri 5.0

Eddy's minions mark th-5period—*ife*, a *forWurn*
of anic root *da*. Salvador Dracu, I presume, sub
to the threshold of a pastry coque? Hola Wassily,
are you the Sode? No, Kemosabe, only a (bi) Epi
of Sode is here to bear witness to th-5period. Me,
you putrefaction, me? I'm just *torted*. Eddy's gut
is lick not tort. *C'est de moi qu'il s'agit dans ce
portrait*. One months later, X-Peri devours th-5p.
Dead are the rating scales. Dead are confessions.
Dead is the place of was. Lives R. Mutt aroused
by Rrose Sélavy, two she-puns of lust, sucking
on cubes of sugar and marble. Sepiidae, my pet,
drain my mania to oops. Eddy depends on you,
or the leather jackets of his ur-sexed restroyer.

Orgasmos 1882

Luv cums in the church—*simbi* (oses), ir/reach, arch
to my touch: skin of *exo* and *artho* engrave pre/post,
a neolinguistics of Mr. Port, Ms. Mant and Ms. Eau.
Gut the central cast. It's a *femme* trinity gamer BRA.
Abracadabra my little zebrafishes. How to misbrand
the bravura with braze? They are sickened, outbrag
the punch hole's brawner. The black *brae* is blacker
than *scienza nuova*. The *aca* of *deme* needs a dildo,
a clear jelly-rubber toy with its plastic aroma of PVC.
Silicone is robust as is chrome plated steel. It's *efirm*
of PC mussels. Eddy Dedalus is Le.O'Pinuse Luvar,
a neoprenic butt-plug with faux tail, flare flange ball
beads of a holy sphincter society of ass worshippers.
His sigmoid colon is her *petite mort*-culated pro/sate.

Bokor 1932

Koob, you mortician, hack and peer.to.peer botnet.
You third.party reanimator of Haitian Creole *zonbi*,
and Kongo *nzambi,* admit that Eddy's fetish *zumbi*
is your *vodou.* Duet and a.Coly.te of the Halperins,
Eddy "koobface" Daemon starred in *White Zombie.*
This is the zombie grip of those sick *xmatons.* This
is the spell of the Lugu Henchmen. My, how seX.y
are these undead slaves. K. Eddy settles for a *bokor*
sorcerer hung like an *ouangas.* They drink a puffer
fish on the rocks, toke deliriants genetically grown
from datura. Come to the dry mouth of a rootwork.
Come to see the Houngan and his Mambos render
the Clergy of Mediocrity frocked. Don't feed 'em
salt. B/Eat is beats sucking human flesh and guts.

Adonis 600

Adonis Mazarin is his real name, cues male virility
and symmetry. Swoon at clarities of skin—gauge
beauty and the honeyed baritone. Pre.static H.Um
of grace, manner and V/shaP.ed torso, tA.ll/dark
and scul/pt.Ed symmetry—face/half mirroring he
the day unshaven skin jaw, mouth curved. I/zatio,
Eddy has face. Eddy has Adonis, has good genes.
This valid marker against the Age of Hinge, r/mot
a seduction to proceed. Eat my face, my lips/chin.
In life a *prima copulism* is a pyros relevance. Not.
The rarity of Re.cAll hears the P.ure Lo.V.er. D.Y.
Mazarin lives our organs, lives lolliromp in struts
of climax. A.M.ere loo.que of love. I cc.An here.I.
A Paris, stressors suck off panic disorder. Eddiiii.

Mediocrity 2.7

Prim indirection Mortimer. I love the spadework. I love
shlimazl, a Gauloises-smoking Parisian flâneur. Morty
was named Alban Pert, the bumper, lover of lyre I/us.
A *roma* of *tics* suffers later syndromes of Isaiah Berlin.
Mock a Blake scape of Wig. How Hershey is/or Eddy?
I am goosed by skin, goosed NSE. Lovy/Romantique,
this French *tur*. Recuse the mock-drama, the hetrials
of posture. Machines of recall guts mediocrity's 2.7
neutered saints—bequeath a stasis. Eddy guts impact
and inheritance. We speak *romantische poesie*. The
wrong transmission. The schlong transmission. Afear
builds a minion. How lame is the rest of your yabled
poetry? How lame is your lap reflex? Annie Louise
Germaine de Staël-Holstein conjures a mafia of N/A.

Icon 1700

Com the Cond of Sus *isen* from *rist*. Dead believers
tag the *rected* from the Lord of Air. In the *ical* book,
Eddy "Thessa" Daemon hears eared *econs* as *pretrib*
left behind. *Surre* me a lovely famme to put in place
of blog trolls. The Risty Rets concoct foppy mirages.
Will they eschew the Ologs with canted crowds? Ols,
Rets, or the gamey mighty, cringe and fret. *Raptus re*
returns to carry off these *turas*. Never mind the *Koine*
Greek of taken. Never mind the *harpazō* of Corinth.
How sweet, stir whir, are these betched slips? Sweet.
Very sweet. Virility's whipcrack will never fumble.
Thessa Eddy lives to love women. No recall as *reve*.
No *rapiēmur*. Pick *parousia*, not *ousia*. Quck these
italics mocking the normanics of relief seek *thera*.

Jest 1996

Primitive *acursen* are to blame. They lay down an enfilade
of same, trying to mollify. He is they as a balletic player's
antiseptic glow. He is to contrive and why not two subsets
of culture? It's high-resin taboo like a harelip on a *Grecian
Urn*. Why name the chump Tapu, to defend inviolate Eddy
"Tapu" Daemon from the high mediocres. His refrigerator
makes cloudy, crescent blocks tossed in a glass with seltzer
and corn vodka. Tapu will be cured by mania, then excess,
then by eyes pierced in slack folds. Decorum is tossed out.
Why all these disincentives and protocols of control? Out
repeat the Stag of Nate in the addict's mouth. Not malady,
and certainly not the punctured balloon of drudgery. New
is now no longer a dark, shiny case of homage and dread.
New is the insectile click. New is the cannibal tag. Relive.

Hewoma 2.8

Suck the slick sleek of the genital tract, the pastiche
of hymen, gloss of leathered vulva. Madame Urethra,
I love you with your silky clitoral hood. Eddy's knees
buckle in, making those dry, sticky *inexoreotic*-saliva
sounds. Nostalgics convene to share Byzantine erotica.
How can the pejorative clauses of Zero Coke talk racy
mosaics? They can't. Future resistances will be quaint.
They will moan with argyle hoods. Argyle? No, Snoop
Dogg apparel from DOGG POUND GANGSTA/SERI
OUS PIMP PENDANT. Madame Urethra in snapback
hat. She's a lil thug, swag phone. U and E of *cloaca*. F,
ert me *facation*. Sex is never safe. Nuthin' but a thang.
Nuthin' but the arch of labia. Comp/da mudder jucker.
Stop monotremes—DFW/Franzen, punk care/human.

Duchess 415

Duchess Marie of Public Alley 415 has Eddy glammed
and clamoring for redness: *gentil*, high-born, manorial,
to bear a coat of arms, an escutcheon, plumed in class
and noblesse. *Très Riches Heures du Duc de Eddy*. He,
among the royal enablers, he as *homo novus* or *homines
novi*. More titles: vassalage, suzerain, fief. Passer/words.
Testimony of the fiber/optic/chest—scaled-up, porcelain
highend and toxic elegant. This *bourgeois gentilhomme,*
this *gentelise*, this *fin'amor,* loves Eddy. Teleputerized.
Never stifle the Co/e.d zones of the uN.awaRdEd new.
We, we Provençals hear neologs as a pastiche of castle
life. Aquitaine, Provence and Champagne are Chicago,
New York and Boston. 1099's first crusade is 2015's.
Marie Champagne, is/or Marie of Back Bay. She/be.

Maillot 1895

Mata hire. Mata firing squad. Mata X/otic, espion.
Eddy's bashert is Margaretha Geertruida Zelle. Ad,
Ad/ma Zelle has nothing on née twisted. Hat shops
for Antje van der Meulen—flirt with a godmother.
The Dutch East Indies' captain is looking for Wife.
July 11, 1895, Amsterdam—leggy C.on/Cu.B/ines.
Dance the eye of day. Dance the con of man. Here,
Eddy is Gabriel Astruc. Here, Mata is a pole dancer.
Mata, the bodystocking, fishnet pantie of raw waist,
scrunched up and put on in the same way as the leg.
Eddy's one-piece aspect is an illusion of nudity. He,
Ancienne Belgique. Eddy's family died in bodysuits.
The hooks of velcro never meant to hurt you. One's
wear is a onesie with crotch snaps, she or/us maillot.

Ascent 30

Eddy is placed in an ossuary, cinemo-optical praxis written
on his skull. The gratis of export. Kiss the relic—metal-cast,
oil jar, wiki beeswax, to burn clean, blood-fed—just neural
spasms. He unscrews the urgent to climb *Ladders of Divine
Ascent.* Eddy writes the new Syriac *Doctrine of Addai.* 30
rungs. He presses the cloth to his wet face. We have drawn
a dead likeness of the dead with 3 disposable shrouds. We
are hell's rubber vacuum. We are province kneeling before
h.im/a.liVe.in/H.eaV/e.n. Eddy, stagger, lunge, commune:
yellowed at the stem, upturns generations to an *anchoress.*
Eddy's cell in Skipton is cloistered in the gland. A shade
infects to the purity of teeth and hair. Our wingspan balls
the void. The last virgin is consecrated. Is Eddy's tongue
a summons to hear the dead? This is his talent to live up.

Dormition 15

Saint Eddy "aureola" Daemon is oval-shaped, his *vesica piscis* limned against the screen, decorated by *quatrefoil* with its patina of four-lobes. Aureola Daemon is a glory. His future is emitted backwards from a *Brocken Spectre* cast in the low sun. He beauties *The Glory of the Pilot.* E.M.A.nation from the headed light, plus triptych vites. Comes down to these mandorlas in the coaxial medulla. H.R.I.st in his majesty. Please stop the quip: dormition of the mother feast is not fixed in a date. Nativity fasts are faster than fish, oil and wine. How about the least blessing of water? We'll sleep in the cemetery. *Contra antidicomarians* are about a death of the Virgin Mary. No one admits that the crawlspaces are above the false ceiling. Pedantry teaching demurs to the Holy Virgin.

Orb 5.2

Eddy weds the Ir/weD.ded Irene of Thessaloniki. Licinius couples the core of a cold-fusion ring. The Father broken in pieces, reassembles as a lithioid. St. Seraphim of Sarov begs the dramaturgy. Penelope's beauty is hydrocephalic in heavy rinds of ancient flesh. She is trampled by horses, wifi laced behind her head. Suffer the dread miracle, the atrophic neck of divine heads. Thousands convert. Graves are found emptied of gravestones. She never died. Come on down and ad-lib the cachectic. She does little to settle into sulcus. Why would she, when the creator's right hand is stained? Ed.D.y's a Facebook like in Saint Irene. She's a somnambulist in the 4th century of 2015. An idol father lives again in the blurred ellipse of subways, raised back to life by the *aptize rayer*. Fantods chant as she walks up.

Bunjie 5.1

Now, a *Commedia all'improviso* of Eddy "Bunjie"
Daemon and his kilowattage specs—kitchen-rigged
shivs with the b/bells of the stock detachable Punch,
grossly exaggerated as A.c/K jongleurs with a beak
nose. Knee-slap his acromegaly, d/R.essed in black
with rasp and swazzle. No tantrums, mate, of facial
isometrics. Carry around macaroni, wooden spoons
and peaked hats in your manpurse. He squirm zanni.
He publics the raw, unalloyed, agendaless kindness.
Click on the lowered center of gravity, back arched,
knees bent, toes pointed. Then re/Vide—hY.phenate.
Elbows, ladies, arms half lifted like a zonni jubilant.
Dear Bunjie, take a sonnet or gut the *intox* of *cated*.
We of pancreatitis-flare, keep the *burlas* of Q.Judy.

Te./po 5.4

Eddy hums the teppered beauty pageant, the *rayonnant*
of rose windows—he the *bellitas*, he the Bunjie Jumper
of the Abyss. He.bellus—he, the hair style of M.EtIc.S.
His skin is almond, lily, cumin—the honeyed lime soap
of male lipstick. Eddy wanders in fimme. Golden ratios
become taut with iodine and bromide. Drama aims for
virility, the virility of the su.Bl.om/e—soft, licked: make
her ache for the last M.an. The index and thumb of here
charisma, skin smooth, overlaid with the waisthip ratio.
Hourglass figures are poles abutting pubis and breasts.
These eye-corners of climax—these flexing pectorals:
mO.re/Ye.t to.Com.E for Eddy's divine us. Susanna.l.
ot.U/s as Susan of Inshushinak from the root bean
of *nucifera*, lakebed water garden, humming *ower*.

Pook 5.3

Gloria in *excelsis deo*, doxo of angels, has overturned
the hat. A handsome zombie as a Nosferatu hottie? It
picks a noir of *idiotici*. The card's lyric *te duem*, now
relives as *phos*. Caper less than expect living to serve
and dissect. Frustum-shaped? No, just a *vetus*, hearing
the leaking of lysergics. I done the elongated babble. I,
the She of Goof, stand cradling the broom of *terra pax*.
Hear the sung rubric, spirit free to projectile vomit the
less/than/easy submitted down-double of no reprieve.
How about those lented votives of confession? Write
the prepare. These caulked Paragons of Insincere. Yes,
because a party is a awake to dangle vivids. She press
an Eddy button. She rather prefer to all-include. No,
to balk vacuums. Yes, Bunjie says ego-raws goodbye.

Lefe.ty 917

Cross-sectioned wakes throw away her paraphilia. Not prophet Daniel, but the burnt acetate of Lady Delphina. Or.al N.oR u.d of a future much farther than the caged sincere. Is it the beard matted in less than the pubic-black of regret? D.Eaf this jested cur. You stomached to radicalize bad posture are our bloc\ked shadow of light—opaque among *antumbra*, sunspot the dark I of circular cones. How sack and même is its current time? Blah the hemorrhaging for.Ge/t. No one cares the place, era—mode. In the apex of the circular cones, clones of the umbra less are more. Mo.Re is the lessed coeur. Eddy is openly empty of fra time, hearted less to reveal the weak drudgery of continue. He wills the Agon of Fight. Cum-giants of will/live.on continue. They let Eddy star in the past camera. Why? Why the idioms of a horrid reminder? Because smoke is the ash of a tray/ED.

Man 1480

To mock Sir Frank Bernard Dicksee's fashionable wamen,
is to mock the variants of symbiosis—facie my spe.cie. Fi.
Aga.PE, A.M/ong theus, continues to shun a/P.ath.y. S.he
of the trasted U.ve, scatters the She of Resolve to W/ri.T.e
the very last L.U/v. How strong is the last love of empty?
Enough to withstand the dead of your recall. M'et me, I'm
the new poetry. Quip the p/mathy. Not this time you cares
theories of not. These Narcis of C.R.oss quit some U/nr.e
of a traditional harem. How hungry is the thirst of E.ntry?
No god demurs. No religio demurs to our romance. *Helios*
of a *zentrik* 674 x 958 (186.496 Byte). How the *uck* of *nar*
bores the plenty of these ones who won't post or L/I.k:E?
Ro, beauties, r.Re/.v.Olt. Hear da .luv of undead lust. We,
kiss da skin A.x. E.d/y kiss our lovely lips. Beauty. U.T/y.

Flatliners $3e^{i\pi/2}$

The last drop of salvia's social berth—x.tatic, concave
and in the bone-box of brain heaving—enter flatliners:
asshats of asystole and jelly doughnuts. How semiotic
is jelly? A t.ad less signifier than double-chocolate rum
cake. They creep back. Sal Dracu and Orb Oran a barb
head *Di./um* as the new crime of invention. It's *X-Peri*
in lacquer, porcelain and pewter. We lied. The to.w.el
rack is fiber optic. Frivolity is not for the faint-hearted.
To catapult past the brain death of the quo is to decamp
the rot and gag it with zero intent. Move mobile. Retox.
Cover palimpsest with toilet paper and coat with matte
finish. Today, Eddy straps on the et cetera of scissors.
We have become the cannibals of the canon, r.eco.ns
of snort, cropped as Señor Wences' lipsticked thumb.

Stem 200

C.u/T the *mi* from the marriage of *tosis* and macramé
and get danglers who leave early and go back. Prog.e
or nit.ors? Nothing like a day away in sensory triage.
We're here to replenish adult tissue, as with any cell
turn.oVer/ed to live. The yesterday p/O.em has been
mugged and beaten. Blood-skin rejuvenates E.lbows.
We, as one among the induced pluripotent, p.L.e./X
at your intimidating size. Hey, M.Auto Logous, Eddy
missed his curfew. They remember the prex-peri.ali
period drilling into the bone of femur and lilac crests.
How weak is their advice to give a prompt? Adipose
requires blood be drawn. Memes are our contextuals:
self-renewal is a glassy overhead. This c/onVocation
is our potency. *Tenabrae factae sunt*. Rupt da jackal.

Tika 91

Bull terriers on chains, gladiators in x.charis: alerters
of *crux gammata*, unicode U+534D, serving former
servers—you are the 20-sided polygon of Pee Tika.
The Daughter of Arp says it's in the edges of reeds,
in a square basket-weave Pee Tika used to pr./ot.O
wr.it/e the ecliptic pole. Help us. These tetradic 4s
are renotes sucked through the bloody *curculi*. Gag
me Tika with the s.wa of your magen force. Square,
cross, cube—red, white, black, later distilled a pure
cyan—steal shape and thickness conferred on grace
and favor. Here's our ultraman. You wouldn't think
so, but Eddy is Gathas seducing re.ocents. A triune:
Gathas, Tika and The Daughter of Arp—some/on.e
has to work in our family—über replaced by m.E/ta.

Intromit 7.9

Radix. Corpus. Glan. Two corpora. Meatus and balls
of a baton-twirler—armored or testosteroned, groped
by the lardy tubist with pucker lips. Bulb and crus vie
for the *ineal* pouch of a new era: The Age of Posteros.
His hirsute torso is post-gender and *polis*-soiled. Post
the post-phobic theory to retire the form with a thrust.
E.vent/s are pathological. No *frenum* here, the gland
submits to the prepuce. Wear a chinstrap for Eddy's
digital *juvenilia* bomb—a photo bomb, a duct: hum.
He, his bicuspids, renege on the death of pleasure. I
spin make. I am a fan/act.ic, worshipping the E.fertil.
Choice is dead. Post Me! Dead Me yourself. Monitor
me because I tra.Vars your stir an U.r of Queef. Hell
me game-changer. E.Raphe me you *isible* stud. Beat.

Patina Fe$_2$O$_3$·nH$_2$O

Ed.rots the red oxide to redox the flaky, the friable, unlike any patina. The c.orR.osion of iron, murders these feeble edits of rust. Kill the E/.d>itor>s. They maximize Maximil.ian, because Max.imil.ia is lust, pure lust of an opportunist, x.cused to receive flesh texts. E. mips an underwater concrete pillar, rebars the strength of a weakening bond. Corrosion loves the dissi.milar e./wa/y. Re.rites—the Gram of Mar. Re.rites—the p.o/et/ry murders. Corrodes the alloy of combine and bitch smacks zombies of yorticold coractness. River sludge the r.ats our ferric clichés. Wack their gonads with chairlegs. Mak.Um shriek. Mak.Um beg for an end to bloody skin. The Muse of Sulfur Dioxide exposes a future of I.ron B.allet.

Extinct 3079

Extinct in the schema of status, sub-reliant as a s/u.c
of c/ess, gummed by *tinct*, Eddy's data is de/fic.ie.nt.
How *leasty* is the *cern*? Quite robust, thanks to a.s/k
groping for the crit/s. Is E.d.d/y a Carolina Parakeet,
neotropical in size and coloration to extant jendays
and sun conures? His plumage is green with lighter
green underparts and bright yellow headed *dorange*
forehead. This high risk of en.da won't now vintage
hemorrhage its authentic confession. Our E./s.>i<S
has been liberated. Don't "shoot shovel or shut up."
Over-hunt the game of limit to reanimate invasives.
No crease. No resistance. Conserves balk at captives.
Dholes are canid natives. This one's about parakeets
and dhoels. This one's about a gene pool of lovlies.

Kippur 5776

Eddy once gagged on the bane of *kippur* to skin the seal
of verdict. Vid./ui hombre, to jerk a confession. How far
back are we from the vein-laced head? Far. Unforgiven.
We hear your thiamine stink. How far will you s.o.A/r?
Redemption is degenerative. These Lords of Topspeed
promised to afflict our souls—the Shabbat of Sabbaths.
How strict is our day of rest? The five names of dread:
soul, wind, spirit, living one and unique one, haunt E.d
No eating. No leather. No showers. No aftershave. No
sex. Cop an edenic e.xp/ul and stack polystyrene cups
in the locked closet. Re.t.U/R.n E/.d to a pristine state.
It all resets in the force of the body. Sundown/nightfall,
Icarus-eyed from a caffeinated two-day blackout. Fast.
Don't waiver. Cede. Be the arity of the arced E.>.v.>e.

Golem 139:16

Po.mor/ph as *gamli* of an unshaped form, me the Hu
of Ods, unfinished, uncultivated, dumb in *pless*, lunk
goylems as a bundle of dish. How brainless is Clum?
How far can the poesis be stretched beyond the other?
The clumsy demand attention, the way dust demands
to be kneaded into a shapeless husk. Mud is created
by those close to divinity and unable to speak. Jests
are neither sudden nor infinite. They nod in rows. He
creates a man out of a thousand *shems*. Our foreheads
mouth deactivation to re/m.ove the split. Pull out. Go
when you're sucked over. Reverse the law of creation.
Please sort our current before it mingles a mare-code.
Eddy loves the feed of speed. He tags his ancestry. He
names no progeny, but the Holy Scar of the N>am<e.

Ham 1602

Re.a/m the n.de/ad: re.a/am the F/lesh of Agic. Me.thod
me your virus. Surgence. Surgent. Living the dead glow
of a living dead—staple the art, staple glambi of/or ham.
Seize me da throne. Seize me Am./leth the Predec. Luv
me or saxo./gram me the brain bits. First, or x.uck four
quartos. Second, he palls for the plot device. S/.crutiny:
rampart-nights muck the maxim—*ronic*, or for those/he
loves, antic, but not solemnly, nor ultimately e.mpathic.
Eddy's ghosts vanish in his beauty. No heart should be
this power. Two/be, nor not./be/x.t.be/not. Enter a try.
Enter the Mute King of Play. Proof is so less than post.
Put the rival pour into a *tuck* of *urgat*. Make noise. She
leaves the drag. She *execut*. Pick return, sisters. P./i.CK
the *cerbate*. E is sorry. Genius is Bight. Frogile. Aternal.

Glossolalia 927

Bu./rr.ow, to form as predation and temporary refuge
in the hermetic lair. Ed.y conjures Orb, the Stellarina.
For slr.ep deprivation. Loco my motion, fe.stas. Loco
the dimensions of my total length. Simple tube a few
centimetres long to a complex network. Amphibians,
dragonet, lungfish, sea urchins, crustaceans or clams:
Eddy lives to sit on hemorrhoid-hostile folding chairs.
Orb speaks for Eddy's lagomorphs. Known burrowers
recoil from every lame reference to F./z K.fka, or W/S
Shakes, Tartar gatekeepers. Figur/r.out, y. R.seed now.
Speak T/O/N/G/U/E Ms. Glos S. Olalia, tongue of Orb,
the Stellarina. Eddy's a xenogloss, avatar of Salvador
Dracu. The blood moon is a man/.neq.uin: a bluroid
of pitch and charm, tosses the raptured back to black.

Alchemy 1606

Cameo by The Megisti, metal-pedaled, less flummoxed
by his damaged noble copper and mercury, but still lit
with spewed vitriol—conferred in longevity, prostrate,
throbs gaily and takes Panacea Avenue to i.m>mo.r./t.
Gno ennobles the *eso* of *exo*. The Movement is A./foot.
Endangered Posters have been accused of charlatanism,
prone to inciting photic seizures in the leisurely classes.
Eddy Megisti returns to strut a homey, post-human split,
to give x-peri.verse the muscle of a future signal crowd
from the po.dium. Histic's agree: it's Bolus of Mendes
and tip Eddy Megisti. Both are deprogramming norms.
Both remix brines and aqueous solutions with caffeine.
The Periodic Tables shouldn't sex a leather jacket. By
whom, asks a listener? Any listener, or a feared optica?

Offspring F1

E./d may yet be known as a brood, a chick shatched from a clutch of eggs, spring.s an off of mate. E.dd/s children are the f1 generation, in which gametes fuse and form prophets of offspring. He worships post/ed postures, pinched into off./exact duplicates: chin off the chest of an attitude of self. This history of a false name launches vessels. The starship "Linkage," oves the prove. Father Eddy Meiosis at your service: let us hear the genes and remove the nucleus. Care for rare tungsten light? No. Libate the late Age of Extremes. Libate the Late Age of Tipsy. Libate his teenybopper b-movie croon. Wearing promoters aren't dangerous. The public layer. The no./force lair. Pick either. We guild the lily. We sport bling fedoras. We offsprung.

Daniel Y. Harris is the author of 9 collections of poetry and collaborative writing including *The Underworld of Lesser Degrees* (NYQ Books, 2015), *Esophagus Writ* (with Rupert M. Loydell, The Knives Forks and Spoons Press, 2014), *Hyperlinks of Anxiety* (Cervena Barva Press, 2013), *The New Arcana* (with John Amen, New York Quarterly Books, 2012) and *Paul Celan and the Messiah's Broken Levered Tongue* (with Adam Shechter, Cervena Barva Press, 2010; picked by *The Jewish Forward* as one of the 5 most important Jewish poetry books of 2010).

His poetry, experimental writing, art, and essays have been published in *BlazeVOX*, *The Café Irreal*, *Denver Quarterly*, *E·ratio*, *European Judaism*, *Exquisite Corpse*, *Levure littéraire*, *Milk Magazine*, *Moria*, *The New York Quarterly*, *Notre Dame Review*, *The Other Voices International Project*, *Otoliths*, *In Posse Review*, *The Pedestal Magazine*, *Poetry Magazine*, *Poetry Salzburg Review*, *Stride*, *Tarpaulin Sky* and *Ygdrasil*, *A Journal of the Poetic Arts*. He holds an M.Div from The University of Chicago and is the Editor-in-Chief of *X-Peri*. http://x-peri.blogspot.com/